THE
FEMALE ANCESTORS
OF CHRIST

A C.G. JUNG FOUNDATION BOOK

The C. G. Jung Foundation for Analytical Psychology is dedicated to helping men and women grow in conscious awareness of the psychological realities in themselves and society, find healing and meaning in their lives and greater depth in their relationships, and live in response to their discovered sense of purpose. It welcomes the public to attend its lectures, seminars, films, symposia, and workshops and offers a wide selection of books for sale through its bookstore. The Foundation also publishes *Quadrant*, a semiannual journal, and books on Analytical Psychology and related subjects. For information about Foundation programs or membership, please write to the C. G. Jung Foundation, 28 East 39th Street, New York, NY 10016.

THE FEMALE ANCESTORS OF CHRIST

ANN BELFORD ULANOV

SHAMBHALA
Boston & London
1993

Shambhala Publications, Inc.
Horticultural Hall
300 Massachusetts Avenue
Boston, Massachusetts 02115

9 8 7 6 5 4 3 2 1

First Edition
Printed in the United States of America on acid-free paper ♾
Distributed in the United States by Random House, Inc.,
and in Canada by Random House of Canada Ltd

Library of Congress Cataloging-in-Publication Data

Ulanov, Ann Belford.
The female ancestors of Christ/Ann Belford Ulanov.
—1st ed. p. cm.
"A C. G. Jung Foundation book."
Includes bibliographical references and index.
ISBN 0-87773-939-0 (alk. paper)
1. Jesus Christ—Genealogy. 2. Tamar (Biblical figure)—
Psychology. 3. Rahab (Biblical figure)—Psychology. 4. Ruth
(Biblical figure)—Psychology 5. Bathsheba (Biblical figure)—
Psychology. 6. Psychoanalysis and religion. I. Title.
BT314.U53 1993   93-402
221.9'22'082—dc20   CIP

for

RUTH PINE BELFORD

and

ANNELIESE AUMÜLLER

CONTENTS

THE
FEMALE ANCESTORS
OF CHRIST

ONE

WHY THESE WOMEN?
WHY THESE FOUR?

NOTHING ODDER OR more stimulating occurs in the genealogies of Christ's ancestors than the appearance of four women: Tamar, Rahab, Ruth, and Bathsheba. There are only two genealogies of Christ's ancestors, Matthew 1:2–17 and Luke 3:23–38, and only Matthew includes the four women. Why does Matthew place them among the "begats," which for the rest consists only of men and the lines of fathers? Why only these women? And why only four? What is special or distinctive about them? And why have we heard so very little about them in our traditions and our teachings? What explains their presence in the Tree of Life leading to Jesus?

These four women are the female ancestors of God. They help bring Christ into the world. They prefigure Mary. They are part of the great mothers of our religious history. Why have we heard so little about them? I propose to examine the four ancestresses, to bring to their presentation in Scripture the resources of depth psychology in order to explore the symbolic meaning they carry for the feminine and its bearing on our understanding of Christ.

But before we can ask about this quartet specifically, we must ask about the genealogies in general. Why do these "begats" exist in our sacred texts? What are the authors trying to accomplish? And do they succeed? Don't we all just skip over all those "begats" when reading the Bible, and when was the last time we heard them read in a service of worship?

From a theological point of view, the concern of genealogies with genesis, with origins, establishes Jesus as a figure stretching from the beginning of all things up to the present. Matthew traces Jesus back to David, the great king of Israel, and through him to Abraham, the father of the faith. Luke traces Jesus through David all the way back to the beginning in Adam as the son of God, thus establishing Jesus at the source of the human. Both Matthew and Luke establish that Jesus belongs to the house of David, Matthew tracing Jesus' lineage through David's son Solomon, and Luke through Nathan, who, like his brother Solomon, is a son of David by Bathsheba. As David's sons they belong to the tribe of Judah, and so in ancestry does Jesus.[1]

Linking Jesus with David accomplishes several important things. It emphasizes Jesus' solidarity with all of humanity, through David's connection with the father of the faith, Abraham, and through Adam's with the Father God. It links the two testaments. Christ and the new covenant spring in the blood as well as in the faith from Yahweh's covenant with Israel. Although Jesus referred to himself as Son of Man rather than as Son of David, thus making associations less fixed and less narrowly nationalistic than David's and emphasizing his humanity and his coming in humility, nonetheless the Davidic descent of the Messiah is always assumed in the New Testament. Matthew and Luke establish through their genealogies that Jesus was born God's son and the Davidic Messiah from birth. Jesus enters Jerusalem, in his passion as the Son of David (Matt. 21:9), and Paul constantly stresses the Davidic ancestry. Thus is the new Messiah linked with the originating forerunner Messiah in the Hebrew Bible. David's house was to last forever. When the fall of the temple and the exile occurred, the Prophets looked to the reestablishment of the full sovereignty of David as central to the deliverance of the nation. As hope for the Messiah grew, it was thought that it would come from the house of David. The genealogies of Jesus place him in that royal line, so that gathering around him the traditions and hopes attached to the expected Messiah they help define what it was his mission to fulfill. David is his ancestor, the one who goes before; the Jewish Messiah forecasts his coming, the law his bringing of the spirit.

From a psychological point of view, these genealogies bring to consciousness all the complexes of the psyche that our ancestors represent. Complexes are emotionally charged clusters of ideas and images grouped around an archetype. They tell us not just where we have come from but what exactly the collective unconscious may present to us through the psychic constellation that we must contend with as symbolized by our ancestors.

We will see this specifically in what the four female ancestors bequeath to Jesus, which, like much of the feminine aspect of religious life, has been greatly neglected in our study of theology and Scripture. When we know the line of our origins, we symbolically put before our egos the lineage of complexes, what Marie-Louise von Franz calls our "total family of complexes," which directly affects our span of life.[2] Such knowledge allows us to live consciously, not having to dissociate, repress, or fall into violent identification with a complex.

Living in touch with what our ancestors symbolize in the emotional contents of the unconscious allows us to see that we live as part of a greater whole. Our ego, specifically that "I" at the center of consciousness, discovers, as von Franz puts it, "that this whole economy of the household is ruled by another center, namely the Self."[3] This discovery relieves the ego of the burden and aggrandizement of thinking it must manage all the complexes by itself, to be their ruler, so to speak. In fact, it is the Self, that center of the whole psyche, conscious and unconscious, that rules over the psyche and quietly (often secretly) regulates the whole system. When the ego is in touch with the Self, it too knows about those other complexes. The stress in the genealogies upon Jesus' connection to David suggests that in the Hebrew Bible David was the accepted Self-symbol. The coming of Jesus as the Christ introduced a new image of the Self, one in firm connection to the old, indeed growing out of it. All the more important, then, to ask about the four women who turn up in the New Testament genealogies of Jesus. What elements of the feminine do they carry over from the Hebrew Bible into the new being disclosed in Christ? What complexes of the feminine—of energy, imagery, and affect—are thus put in touch with this new revelation, perhaps to be included in religious life for the first time?

Delving into this connection of new and old offers still more psychological understanding of the genealogies. If we know who our ancestors are, we can live in unbroken continuity with the past. That in turn grounds us in the present, protecting us against being blown this way and that by every new wind of religious fashion or political movement. Continuity roots us in something beyond our own time and nourishes our sense of dignity and duty in living creatively with what tradition has bequeathed us. Just as we can entertain our different complexes imaginatively and thus protect ourselves against psychic splits and dissociations, so our culture in honoring our ancestors may connect what we were with what we are and may suggest what our children may become. Von Franz puts it strongly: the ancestral genealogy of Christ symbolizes the "integrated personality who has the whole past development of the past . . . behind him, as if the whole past pointed to his birth and reality."[4]

Sometimes genealogies even include animal ancestors. The animals circling the figure of Christ in Christian mandalas offer one example. Ox, eagle, lion, and human person surround Jesus at the center and thus depict the divine as rooted in the instinctual, the spiritual as rooted in the material and the human. The presentation of the Christ in human form, like the man in the mandala enclosure, insists that it is in the human person that the new Self will be born.

Examining the four female ancestors of Christ, we can imagine a second mandala, composed of their four figures and Mary as a fifth woman, at the center, holding the divine babe at her breast. These women surround Jesus' beginnings, just as the gathering of all the Marys accompanies his ending on the cross and receives his transformation in the Resurrection.

Looked at causally, a genealogy gives a vision of the originating source from which we can trace a line of development to our present life, to this day. Looked at prospectively, a genealogy enables us to ask what will be breaking in upon our present life from the future.

Von Franz links the meaning of genealogies with Jung's idea of synchronicity.[5] When we experience a meaningful coincidence of events that display no causal connection, we glimpse a bigger world where all things connect to make a whole. This is a kind of knowing that brings simple certainty. It operates beyond our usual ego-knowing and brings, says Jung, a kind of "absolute knowledge" that comes from its links to the collective unconscious.[6] Von Franz cites the example of a primitive people that know through this channel that a rhinoceros will be coming along a path, say in ten minutes, a fact essential to survival that it could not know by rational means. We can think of comparable situations where we discern facts of vital importance by some mysterious means that exceeds our rational knowledge. We need this other kind of knowing, symbolized by the ritual of ancestral continuity, because it opens to us the absolute knowledge of the unconscious, which we, like people in a primitive world, need for survival.

Looked at causally, the four female ancestors of Jesus show the long-omitted female elements that insist on being included in our lives and that in their acceptance secure the line of David. This suggests that Christ as the new Messiah will bring with him not merely acceptance but willing inclusion of the female elements of being.

Looked at synchronistically, the four female ancestors establish a psychic field around the coming figure of Christ, each making visible concrete individual aspects of the cosmic whole. Each female figure organizes in her story inner and outer factors that will be part of the totality of Christ. Together, these women make visible a whole range of feminine actions and responses, initiatives and presence, perseverance and devotion, housed within the saving revelation of Christ. To receive Christ, then, is also to receive feminine elements very different from the meek and mild sweetness by which Mary has been identified by some dubious traditions.

Genealogies are taken up in smaller ways by depth psychology in its emphasis on the importance of the family tree, the web of conscious and unconscious connections of the tribal clan, the whole pattern of "object relations" on which we depend for birth and nurture. To draw our family tree, our genogram, a practical tool in family therapy, we trace our ancestors for three generations, showing their relation to each other and to ourselves. This gives us a succinct picture of the whole family system.[7] Parents can see how they have labeled their son in terms of an uncle ("weak, just the way Julius was") or how their daughter carries the tag that labeled their mother ("bossy, always having to do things her own way").

The genogram provides an immediate image of complex family patterns, making visible major motifs and problems as they evolve and persist from generation to generation. Present conflicts among family members are set within a larger picture of interrelationships of the whole tribe. What never fails to astonish here is the embeddedness of the individuality of persons in a kinship system. We see how inextricably interwoven we are with each other, across years and generations. We see our private and personal experiences of family set within historical events, sometimes across many societies and cultures. The case of a forty-year-old woman gives a small illustration.[8] She had long felt herself rootless in her larger family system, different from every immediate family member, alienated from any identifying tribal ancestry. One thing strongly counteracted her sense of alienation: the quality of space she remembered from her childhood house. There she felt contained, held in being, she said, with a deep sense of belonging. The spatial proportions of the rooms, how they fit into one another, and the great size of the house all sheltered her and made her feel connected to a reality that encompassed her individual self. A professional event offered her an opportunity to journey to see her father's childhood house in a distant state. Public recognition of her grandfather's skill as a builder marked this house as a landmark; a town square was named in his honor. She was stunned by her experience of her grandfather's house, released from alienation for the first time. Walking the rooms, she felt the same quality she had known in her original childhood house of space holding her, permitting her to be, buoying her up. Only then did she focus on the fact that both her grandfather and her father had themselves built their houses. She felt through her pores, through the bodily expe-

rience of moving through the interior spaces of both houses
the legacy of grandfather to father to daughter of a large lived-
in space handed down from generation to generation. She
knew in her skin and bones why the town felt called to cele-
brate her grandfather. For the first time in her life, this forty-
year-old woman felt embedded in a tradition, a history, a
tribe, anchored to a little town thousands of miles from where
she lived. She had inherited from her ancestors an exquisite
appreciation of living space.

This sense of inheritance, of who goes before and bequeaths
such legacies, is what we shall look at in the female ancestors
of Christ. It is a legacy Scripture insists upon, even if we view
it as more symbolic than literal, more mythic than historic.
Just as the woman in her experience felt herself tied to the past
life of her father and grandfather, and to an era in a distant
town's history, through the spatial qualities of their houses,
just so do the ancestresses of Jesus tie him to qualities of the
feminine that enrich his being and shape his revelation. They
contribute much to what comes through Jesus as the Christ.
These ties of Jesus to the feminine link the two testaments, the
two Messiahs, and Jesus with all of us in all of our humanity
back to Adam as the son of God.[9]

By *feminine* I mean a principal mode of being human that
exists in all of us regardless of sex or sexual emphasis, that
involves us in the midst of things rather than at an abstract
distance from them. In the feminine mode of being we tend to
live in a state of identity with other people, or with ideas, or
feelings, and to act by being for them, rather than by doing
things to them. In thinking, we all know what it is to be seized
by a hunch or a vision on the edge of clarity, which we allow
to gestate in us and help bring to birth, in contrast to structur-
ing an idea logically that we can critically examine from a pre-
cise mental distance. Feminine modes bring with them a style

of consciousness that is imbued with unconscious mental processes, in contrast to a masculine style of consciousness that differentiates itself from the unconscious and capitalizes on a process of gathering its perceptions into concise, discrete conscious categories. The feminine styles of spiritual transformation lead downward to despised and rejected parts of life where intensity blazes up; this is very different from a transforming process that leads inexorably upward out of murk into a sharp clarity about what really matters most and defines itself as best.[10]

The genealogies in Matthew and Luke are not accurate historical documents or even consistent with each other. We might better think of them as theological imaginings that contribute to the tantalizing ambiguity surrounding Jesus' birth. For they trace Jesus' lineage through Joseph to his great ancestors but ignore the gap created by the Holy Spirit impregnating Mary. This entire line of paternal ancestry comes to a full stop with Joseph, leaving an arresting gap between human descent and divine intervention!

My interest in the four women in Jesus' genealogy is filled with theological imaginings that lead inevitably to questions about the feminine roots of Jesus' life and work. What do they bespeak? Where do they come from, where do they lead?

But first we must ask why only four women, and why these among all others? These are not great matriarchs like Sarah or Rebecca or Rachel. Though each of the four is a mother in the line of David pointing like an arrow to the arrival of God breaking into history through Jesus, what stands out about all of them is not anything maternal. Rather, they link revelation in Christ to another side of the feminine, less visible, less comfortable perhaps, but one that equips Jesus with the ability to deal with ease with women as remarkable and as odd as his female ancestors are. These women foreshadow something in

Jesus' own rootedness in the feminine and something more in his revelation as the Christ. We remember that Jesus did not patronize women but spoke to them and of them in great signifying parables, about God's action in the world, about the annunciation of theological truths.[11] These four ancestors also foreshadow the anomalous role of Mary, mother of Christ, the one who bears God into the world in such a mysterious marvelous manner. With Mary as the fifth of the ancestresses, the numbers four and five begin to play against each other. Why only four, and then with Mary, why just five? Why these numbers?

Those of us who suffer from mathematical bewilderment and all its accompanying anxieties know abysmal confusion worse confounded when discussion of numbers and their symbolism comes up. Nonetheless, we must proceed, bolstered by the assumption that nothing in Scripture is merely accident. Each item brings rich symbolic meaning if we can open ourselves to it. Number is a basic principle of the universe from which, in one sense, the whole world proceeds.

Number provides unconscious order when it becomes conscious.[12] In the West, numbers represent quantities; they are abstract, structural pieces of a series. In the East, numbers are also symbols; they present order in concrete modes of thinking and doing, signifying a fullness of organizations in time, acting as transient emblems of the inner and outer elements in any given totality. Each number has its own character, a given identity, a just-so precision that streams forth from it.[13] The number four stands for totality, solidarity. For example, in many creation stories the four elements of earth, air, fire, and water were separated at the creation of the world. Jung links the differentiation of the personality to the ability to apply to experience the four psychological functions of intuition, sensation, thinking, and feeling.[14] Four stands forth again and again in the Bible as a number symbolizing completion. Yahweh's name possesses four letters; four rivers flow from Eden; the cross points in four directions. Four corners and four winds frame the earth. Ezekiel's vision of God's glory centers upon four living creatures, and four living creatures appear in the Book of Revelation to stress the conjunction of the human and the divine. Four evangelists proclaim the Savior, and four angels of destruction figure in the Apocalypse. Four symbolizes the earth, the human situation (as in Jung's notion of the four functions of thinking, feeling, intuition, sensation), and the natural limits of totality. Many material and spiritual forms find their model in quaternity.

The quaternity stands symbolically at the dawn of history, as a world-creating deity, not somewhere outside us but as the God present within the human psyche, a fundamental originating image around which the psyche revolves.[15] It is in this sense that Jung speaks of the divine as an archetypal God-image and of the number four as representative of the God-image within us, which he calls the Self. This does not reduce God to a psychic phenomenon. Rather, the Self exists in our psyche as that which knows about God. We often come upon such experiences of the Self in the work of analysis, and those of us who pay attention to our own dreams can add examples. For instance, after a major dream of triangles signaling tremendous psychic upheaval to come (which subsequent events bore out), a woman in midlife awoke with a dream fantasy that announced: "Trinity calling collect. Will you accept the charges?" She, the receiver, made up the fourth in a quaternity of the divine intersecting with the mortal.[16] And in her subsequent crises of loss of health and home it was precisely the intersecting of divine and human that carried her through to a major reorientation and rebirth.

The four ancestresses lead inevitably to a fifth, Mary, the

Mother of God, who stands apart from everyone else in the genealogies, for the lineage of Christ breaks off with Joseph and then leaps over the gap to embrace Mary, who bears Jesus into the world. Despite the long line of "begats" that points like an arrow through history to target the coming of God as a human person into our midst, the motion is stopped with Joseph, who did not father the son; the Holy Spirit of God did. So the four women circle around the fifth, who by one act is lifted above and ahead of all the ancestors. From her line comes the Savior in spirit; in the flesh he descends from two lines, of David and of Adam.

So it is we must ask about this fifth female figure and why the four are set against the fifth. Again a rich number symbolism opens before us.[17] The number five stands as the *quinta essentia*, not a fifth element added to four known ones but a representation of the realized unity of their existence, the center of the quincunx. Thus Mary as mother of Christ centers the four-sided mandala composed of his female ancestors. Five represents a human microcosm, a pentagon formed by outstretched hands and legs, sharing with the circle the symbolism of perfection and completeness. Five is the number of the center and the meeting point of the four cardinal lines that fan out from it and contract to meet it again. In Chinese philosophy five is the principle of the "expanding feminine which brings the spirit into material and spatial manifestation."[18]

Jung examines the mixture of four and five in the symbolism of the Christian Mass. In the Mozarabic tradition, the breaking of the host in preparation for the Eucharist starts with a halving of it, followed by the breaking of the left half into five parts and the right into four. Jung writes:

> The five are named *corporatio (incarnatio)*, *nativitas*, *circumcisio*, *apparitio*, and *passio*; and the four *mors*, *resurrectio*,

gloria, regnum. The first group refers exclusively to the human life of our Lord, the second to his existence beyond this world . . . five is the number of the natural ("hylical") man, whose outstretched arms and legs form, with the head, a pentagram. Four . . . signifies eternity and totality. . . . This symbol seems to indicate that extension in space signifies God's suffering (on the cross) and, on the other hand, his dominion over the universe.[19]

Can we imagine, then, that the meeting of the four female ancestors of Jesus with the fifth, his mother, similarly signifies both a human origin linked to a long line of forebears and a divine begetting by the Spirit through Mary? Such a mixing of the human and divine also symbolizes the coming of the eternal into space and time—the always-was into the ever-present, *now*.

The genealogical imagining of an unbroken continuity from Jesus back to Adam suggests, even if it never expressly states, that we need women for human continuity. These four female ancestors provide it, each of them, just when the continuity threatens to break. Yet none of these ancestresses knows this pivotal role consciously. Only after each one lives her story, and only through her living of it, is it revealed how pivotal she is. She makes connection through being instead of doing. D. W. Winnicott's wistful remark about the sexes is to the point: that man is always one trying to connect, but woman is continuity in herself, always three, always in the "infinite series . . . [of] baby, mother, and grandmother . . ." whether she has babies or not.[20]

At the last break, God jumps in. All of Jesus' forebears halt at Joseph, and his genealogy leaps to Mary as progenitor of the Christ, thus marking the divine intervention that we remark at each recital of the Creed when we say "begotten, not made." With Mary we find symbolized the mystery of God entering history in human form.

God both fulfills the chain of generation to Jesus and breaks it. A large gap appears: the line leading to Joseph does not end in Jesus. God brings his Son into the world when the Angel Gabriel announces her coming pregnancy to Mary. Thus human ancestors do and do not give rise to the birth of God on earth. The genealogical line points clearly enough to the coming God, and then snaps it off, leaving a yawning gap, just as it gets there. The point is that we do not get to God from our side. God steps across the gap, right here in the genealogy at the jump across lines to Mary. So in fact, Matthew, in recording the ancestors of God, should have placed Mary's, not Joseph's, lineage alongside theirs. Was Joseph's lineage chosen instead in order to mark the momentous meeting of the patriarchal tradition with the One who brings new being—and does so through a feminine genealogy that is hidden? Does this meeting mirror what happens in Jesus? For there God breaks in, invades, and totally rearranges the whole situation and every way we think about it, in an atmosphere that mixes mystery and clarity, humanity and divinity, fleshly antecedents and spiritual.

God does not offer an extension of the human genealogy, but defeats it. We are not offered options among which to choose; we are invaded by a liberating reality that changes the whole force field in which we live. God does not discard genealogy but changes it, after crossing the seemingly unbridgeable gap at which it has arrived. God breaks the human continuity and yet brings it to fullest expression by appearing in person, in the flesh. And as a person born of the feminine line—not of the fathers, with the exception of four female ancestresses. God comes into the world through the feminine mode of being human. The mysterious interplay in the symbolism of numbers, between the four ancestresses on one side and the fifth on the other, prepares the ground for the coming of Christ.

The female ancestors are directly united with each other and with the Jesus continuum through motifs that surface, sound, and resound in their separate stories. Like Mary, all of them know irregular unions; all know scandal. Incest, prostitution, betrayal, exile, trickery, and adultery in the four meet the anomalous illegitimate pregnancy of Mary. Audacity, lavish devotion, initiative, determination, and endurance mark the attitudes of all. All prefigure the Christ and stand forth as antitypes in their bringing to the surface what usually hides itself in the darker aspects of the feminine. They teach us that the shady underside is as important in the life of the spirit as the more obviously acceptable virtues, that dependence on God does not mean blind, passive submission but rather the full, imaginative use of everything God gives us and the offering of it all back to God. God uses everything to bring us to our center of being. At this end of our twentieth century, anything that shows more of Jesus' connection to the feminine must be examined, and scrupulously. Jesus as human is male, yet he is also bearer of a large female component, reasonably enough, for Jesus as Christ presides over all that lives in us, male and female.[21]

Point of View

In the pages that follow, I will examine the lives of the four female ancestors of Christ as they are presented in Scripture and attempt a psychological interpretation of the complex of feminine imagery, affect, and meaning each story offers. *Complex* is a word that is usually associated with disturbance, or even pathology. We say someone has a savior complex, for example, thereby indicating one has fallen into inflation by identifying a small human ego with the instinctive energies and archetypal imagery of the unconscious that always exceeds the bounds of human finitude. Thus such persons seem grandiose to a dangerous degree, a danger to themselves as well as others.

However, the word *complex* also designates the way the psyche normally organizes itself. A complex is both conscious and unconscious and is composed of energy, affect, and imagery that cluster around an archetypal image just below the surface of consciousness. These complexes organize our psyche and we do not think of them as pathological unless they act up and disturb our habitual adaptation to reality.[22] Our century has become sufficiently psychological in its collective consciousness that we speak often of our mother or father complexes, for example, meaning by that all the bundles of reactions to our parents as they are in themselves and as we have made them to be in our imagination (becoming what depth psychologists identify as "internal objects").

What complexes of the feminine mode of being human do Tamar, Rahab, Ruth, and Bathsheba symbolize? These are not familiar complexes. They seem almost deliberately to have been avoided in Christian tradition, where in fact astonishingly little has been written about these women. The answer to this question is important to our faith, I believe, as well as to our understanding of the feminine. We have much to learn from bringing into closer association biblical narratives and the reality of the psyche. When we fail to do this, we miss the full impact of Scripture. When we succeed, we deepen our perception of the divine in the human and the human in the divine, while simultaneously recognizing the gap between them, a gap ultimately to be bridged from the divine side.[23]

How do we do this, especially with an eye to the great impact of what we may learn? What actually am I doing here? This is not an exegetical study within the lines of biblical scholarship, designed perhaps to demonstrate one or more of the various methods of interpretation—literary-form criticism, or historical criticism, or sociological interpretation. Though very useful in securing the text, such approaches do not risk enough to make a bridge to us in the living through and understanding of our lives. Nor does studying these biblical figures psychologically mean reducing Scripture to some psychoanalytical formula to prove its veracity. Though useful to the psychoanalytical guild to exemplify theory, too often the psychoanalytical approach imposes a pat explanation on the reader, just as it imposes its formulas on the text.

This study moves carefully between such extremes in what may seem to some an even more fuzzy area. To me it is in fact much closer to life and the life-giving energies, and what may seem fuzzy is simply what must be preserved of the mystery of its awesome subject matter. Alongside the mystery it makes, depth psychology offers a splendid clarity, I think, through its hermeneutical (interpretive) tools designed to increase our own self-understanding as we work to understand others. As Wittgenstein says, as we look to "find our feet with them."[24]

As with the dialogue that occurs at the center of psychoanalytical treatment, the aim of which is to enlarge the intrasubjective space between and within the two participants, so in our discourse with the female ancestors my aim is to increase the space in which these women meet us and bring us news of the neglected mode of the feminine and its bearing on the revelation in the Christ figure.

Psychoanalytical treatment when it works results in an increased liberation from "hypothesized forces of history and society."[25] Our troublesome symptoms become increasingly superfluous because we understand more of ourselves and others and more from our hearts than from our heads. Psychoanalysis has a built-in hermeneutic function to research, to investigate, to describe, to map matters of concern to its subjects. That is its subject matter. The very exercise of this interpretive skill involves the effect of the person doing it on what is done. Analysts talk about this fact as the effect of their countertransference on their perception of a patient's transference.[26] When treatment goes well enough, the space for discourse enlarges, which in turn enlarges the space for subjects to be; as the philosopher of religion and psychology A. Waelhens puts it, the aim of psychoanalysis is "le rétablissement du discours intersubjectif vrai."[27] But none of this happens unless the analyst allows the process to work on himself as well as on the analysand. It is both or nothing.

Those who confine themselves to the exegetical methods of the biblical guild rarely risk this impact on their own subjectivity. Sadly, the same observation applies to the psychoanalytical scholar. By imposing any formula on a text, we must surely evade the text's implosive impact on us. All such approaches remove the investigator from the investigation and thus radically shrink its validity or altogether invalidate it. Just as analysis does not work if analysts keep themselves out of it, so receiving Scripture on its multiple levels cannot work if no attention is paid to its complex and far-reaching impact on the reader. It is when we cannot or will not enter into discourse that we have recourse "to the quasi-naturalistic level," that is, to explanations of the other as mere object.[28] When we allow explanation and prediction to deepen into self-understanding, "the necessity of distantiation and object-ification of the other will become gradually more rare."[29] We grasp the meaning of tradition in exact proportion to our grasp of the meaning of our own world. If we enter this intrasubjective space of conversation in our contemplation of the four female ancestors of Christ—which is to say, the female ancestors of God—we will learn about ourselves as we learn about them. Our hermeneutics then become a way to repair the disturbed dialogue between Scripture and the world at one of its sorest points, where the feminine has been attacked by being effaced.

The feminine belongs to all of us, men as well as women, as a mode of being, of perception, and of apperception. It has been greatly neglected and, for all the rhetoric, particularly in our century. We see its absence translated into discriminatory actions against women, not only in the obvious ways—in pay, promotion, and privilege—but at all levels of society, not the least at the core of psychological and spiritual life. We feel its absence in the sense of the inferiority, and the compensatory rage, that many women suffer about their body-shapes, their ability to assert themselves effectively, their despair about ever being deeply understood by their male counterparts as beings with a defining spirit of their own. We also feel its absence in the attitudes of men toward the presence of the feminine in themselves. Bafflement, impatience, anger, even dread rise up in many men when confronted by imagery of the feminine. They feel caught, frightened, uncertain, demanded of, and almost invariably are driven to shocked resistance.

Any additional information about the feminine would be valuable, but especially as embodied in these scriptural ancestors at the center of religious and spiritual history, because they bring the neglected sides of the feminine beyond all resistances, right within our grasp. Attention to the ancestresses of God in Christ will help us psychologically and spiritually, at the source of our values, religious or otherwise. These figures bring up to our awareness deep impulses in the human psyche and exemplify how they can be lived in the human community. They show us a larger God, not confined by human rules of what is good and right, but a God who is present in what is bad and wrong too, working at the purposes and procedures of redemption.

TWO

TAMAR

TAMAR'S STORY IS told in Genesis 38. Judah of the twelve tribes, son of Jacob, notorious for selling his brother Joseph into Egyptian slavery, leaves his family and joins an Adullamite named Hirah in his country. There Judah marries a Canaanite woman who bears him three sons. The first of these, Er, is married by Judah to a Canaanite, Tamar, the first of the ancestresses in the line of Jesus. Yahweh is displeased by the marriage, condemns Er as wicked, and slays him. Judah then sends his second son, Onan, to marry Tamar and raise a family in his brother's name. But Onan would not have his seed support and enlarge his brother's name, and so, in famous words, "he wasted his semen on the ground." This is the source of the association of "onanism" with masturbation, long thought in religious tradition to be a sin. For his refusal, Onan too is slain by Yahweh. Judah then sends Tamar back as a widow to her father's house, promising that he will give her his third son in marriage when he is old enough. But Judah is afraid that Shelah, his last son, must also perish if he goes into Tamar in intercourse, and so he delays sending the boy to Tamar.

The drama mounts. Judah's wife dies. He mourns for her, then goes with a friend to a sheep shearing, long a festive event. Tamar, a widow in her father's house, realizes that Judah is not going to give her his third son. She removes her widow's weeds, puts on a veil, and goes to sit at a gateway on the road that Judah must pass. Judah, mistaking her for a prostitute, approaches Tamar. "What will you give me?" she asks. "A kid from the flock" is his answer. She asks for pledges: his signet ring, his cord, his staff. He yields all. They join in intercourse and she conceives. Tamar then returns to her father's house. The next day Judah, returning with the promised kid, cannot find her. He asks, "Where is the temple-prostitute who was by the roadside?" (Gen. 38:21).[1] He is told that no such person has been there. He keeps the goat and goes on his way. Three months later Judah learns that Tamar is pregnant as a result of her harlotry. Judah says, "Bring her out and let her be burned!" (Some commentators say that Tamar is the daughter of a priest, for whom the penalty of harlotry is clear—to be burned alive.[2]) Tamar sends back to Judah the ring, the cord, and the staff, with an accompanying message: "By the man to whom these belong, I am with child." Judah recognizes them as his own and must admit, as the text signifies, "She is more right than I, because I did not marry her to my son Shelah." Nonetheless, "never again did he have intercourse with her." Tamar bears twin sons, in another event of high drama. The first boy puts his hand out of the womb and the midwife promptly ties a scarlet thread on the finger, to mark the elder. But he is pushed aside by his brother, who thus emerges first. This last is the direct ancestor of David and of Jesus, named Perez, meaning he who pushes through, the one who makes a break in the wall. It is after this drama is enacted in Genesis that the story of Joseph in Egypt is narrated.

Like ancient geologic strata, the Tamar narrative yields many layers of meaning. Some are so crude, or even shocking, that there are commentators who dismiss the entire Tamar tale as disedifying, unlovely, and without positive content.[3] I differ strongly. Tamar is a woman who takes heroic measures to resolutely follow the law of levirate marriage, where the surviving male must act as husband to the widow and father to the offspring of his brother. But Tamar, badly used by Judah, must resort in the end to unorthodox means to reach her triumph. She is gripped by a sense of her right, her ardent desire, her need, to have a child. The *Anchor Bible* places her, alongside Rachel, as giving the stuff of motherhood to a virile clan.[4] Some Jewish scholars go further, saying the signet, cord, and staff unmistakably refer to the royal Messiah. They say of Tamar that the "text teaches that she would beat upon her stomach and exclaim, 'I am big with kings and redeemers.' " They recognize God in her: "It was the Holy Spirit that exclaimed, 'Through me did these things occur.' "[5]

The first layer of meaning offers Tamar as foreigner, a Canaanite. Three of the ancestresses are foreign to Israel because they were born in other countries. The fourth, Bathsheba, married the foreigner, Uriah the Hittite. These women spring from peoples whose presence in the land antedates the Israelite conquest and whose religion and customs differ from those enunciated in the covenant with Yahweh.

Canaan is both a place chosen by Yahweh for Israel and Israel's enemy, for its people follow different gods. Here matriarchal religion holds sway. Nature with its cycles of fertility is primary, the summoning spirit only secondary, seen as no more than the means to seed the mysterious depths of the Great Mother. Judah has taken himself to this foreign tribe after collusion with his brothers in the envious punishing of Joseph, the favorite son of Jacob (Israel). Some commentators think the Judah-Tamar story was inserted at this point in Scripture, before the Joseph cycle, in order to show Judah in an inauspicious light because of his shameless treatment of Joseph.

Two of Judah's sons marry Tamar, the Canaanite, a fair representative of her homeland and its religion. We can surmise that Yahweh's displeasure with Er and Onan bespeaks a conflict between matriarchal and patriarchal orientations. The central question poses itself here: which will assume precedence, the matriarchal or the patriarchal? Yahweh wants the sexual spirit channeled into the commanding elements of family, lineage, and Israel's future history. Sexuality is to be firmly united with spirituality. But nature religions view sexuality quite differently, as a divine force in itself. Yahweh does not strike Tamar dead, but attacks her husbands. And her third husband is withheld from her because it seems clear he will die too. Could Judah have identified the power of Yahweh with this woman Tamar? Did Tamar, in asserting her feminine instinct to maternity and her right according to levirate law to progeny, effect the linking of sex with spirit, under Yahweh's power, rather than for its own autonomous powers? From a theological point of view, the conflict between Canaanite nature religion and Yahweh's call to Israel centers around the increasing perception of Yahweh as transcendent, above and beyond all human categories. Chief among these categories, one might say, is sexuality. But Yahweh is above sexual deities, possessing neither female nor male characteristics. He is not a male god who needs a female goddess as consort. From a psychological point of view, the archetype of the transcendent god acts as source for the developing patriarchal society (rather than the other way around, which might be the sociological explanation for his role and position). From this point of view, patriarchy flows from a nodal archetypal image emerging from the objective psyche. Yahweh is the image of a generative, radically transcendent God who creates the world and all that is in it, including sexuality and human reproduction, by fiat and by word. Sexuality, then, is part of human creaturehood, not of divine life. The notion of Yahweh as father is metaphorical, not literal, and the metaphor lies precisely in the point of negative comparison: not father to the maleness of God, no more than mother to the femaleness of God; father as command, not as sexual act; father as outside of a natural relation to his people, a father radically transcendent to all creation. This notion of fatherhood is carred further by Jesus when he addresses God in prayer as "Abba," an Aramaic word for father that conveys the trustworthiness of the deity's authority, its intimacy in the midst of its transcendence.[6]

In contrast to nature and matriarchal religions where maleness and femaleness are invariably central components of deity, in Yahweh they are present but transcended. Sexuality is a gift to creation, a positive component of creation; sexuality is part of the creature's life, not the Creator's, and is to be lived through passionately within a larger permanence, not in brief moments, as in the nights of sacred prostitution in the fertility religions; it is extended and prolonged through the years of life shared between wife and husband.[7] With humor, Scripture selects Tamar, native of the land of fertility religions, to use the fierceness of her sexual instinct for maternity to carry through Yahweh's will, linking sexuality to his divine purpose to produce salvation through an unbroken continuity of line of human generations. And yet Tamar, so bent upon motherhood, brings with her alien elements as well, those associated to the feminine but far outside conventional images of woman as wife and mother.

Quickly, in Tamar's story, a deep dark layer of meaning reveals a still more fearful foreignness of woman, the motif of one who slays her lovers. Each of the first two sons who goes into her perishes, and Judah understandably fears the same fate for the third. Thus he must withhold Shelah. On the surface the text simply says that Yahweh slays the brothers because they do not perform intercourse properly; they waste the seed and prevent offspring. Hidden in the text are all the fears about contraception and its consequences—and deeper still, the terror of woman, whose vagina bites and kills. Tamar touches in her story the deepest dread of the alien female from which springs hatred and discrimination against women. All of us, men and women alike, fear her great power. For all of us are utterly dependent upon woman. Our flesh, our psyche, our minds are shaped by her. A drug-addicted mother produces a drug-addicted infant. An AIDS-infected mother produces an AIDS-infected infant. How we experience our mothers in our earliest months of absolute dependence on her and her responses to us, and in our years of relative dependence on her, strongly shapes how we will be within ourselves and with others when we become adults. We bury this dependence in denial, and in denial our terrible fear of the female grows, working itself out in endless discrimination, in debasing inequalities of standing, security, pay, promotion, and opportunity.[8] For many men, fear of the female fastens onto her sexual parts; impotence, abstinence, or revulsion serve as severe psychological symptoms to protect men from the fantasy vagina that threatens to devour them.[9]

For example, a man in his late forties, suffering from lifelong depression and impotence, describes himself as "feeling trapped by forces that have me in a box. So much time has fallen upon it that I can never now be a useful person. I have yearnings to get outside myself and give to others, but I'm trapped. All my options are closed. Suffocation, expressed in sweaty armpits and palms." Yet to come out of the box is to be filled with insecurity, "like a snail forced out of its shell." He connects this force that traps him, but which he also depends upon, with the female. The female container has become a suffocating box, and yet he cannot live without it. Consciously he rejects the female genital organ as "a primeval oozing hole in which you disappear." Still, through unconscious displacement, he finds a way to approach the dreaded female, bolstering his maleness through homosexual bonding. He dreams: "There is a sexy man screwing a woman in my bed. After he has finished he lets me approach him with my hands, which quite thrilled me—like a wild animal allowing itself to be petted. I also felt the bottom of the woman's partly open vagina and enjoyed doing that too."

Another man, in his thirties, one who has withheld himself sexually from his wife, feeling contempt for her body and her sexual approaches, brought two dreams that showed both his dread of the female and his way of attacking her. Before the first dream, he had felt ill, fearful, alone. He dreamt he was back in his childhood home. It is dark and he is sick. A doctor examines him and opens the cheeks of his face surgically. "What exists on the other side of my teeth are shark's teeth!" the dream exclaims. In the second dream, he puts his hand in a dog's mouth, which becomes a woman's vagina. His hand is stuck—he cannot get it back! In these dreams envy and attack of the female vagina join with dread of its power. It represents a frightening mouth that holds one fast, yet the male dreamer's own mouth hides shark's teeth fixed to devour it!

Can we not hear this dread of the feminine in Judah's refusal to give Shelah to Tamar lest he also die after entering her? And after the birth of Tamar's children, which he has fathered, Judah refuses to enter her again. This alien woman brings to the ancestry of Jesus a deeply fixed threat and inspires an unconscious dread of female sexuality. Could this be something that Christ redeems?

What in fact must be redeemed is the full range of men's fears of being devoured by the female. One such fear fastens onto the vagina, as we have seen. Another affixes itself to a woman's wish to bear a child. Tamar goes to every length to accomplish this goal. In Israel, her story reminds us, a married woman's primary obligation was to bear children, and especially male ones.[10] Fruitfulness was a blessing, barrenness a curse.

Some women today still carry a similarly fierce conviction that only in bearing children will they know fulfillment. They bear on a personal level what ancient Israel bore culturally. Biologic instinct joins psychological obsession. Sometimes, as in illegitimate teenage pregnancy, where children bear children, it may be because a girl feels empty and worthless in herself; a baby kicking inside her fills the emptiness, makes her feel altogether alive. For older women, married or unmarried, conscious and unconscious factors may join in the obsession to become pregnant. They may be trying to repair a damaged body- and self-image, proving by the production of a healthy baby that they have goodness inside themselves from where the babies issue. They may be trying to make reparation to their mothers by giving a grandchild, or to achieve status in their families and society by adding to the family tree, or to give something to their husbands, or to give birth to themselves again through their babies, or through their children to repair their own unhappy childhoods. Pregnancy can be used to secure a faltering marriage, or to force a wedding. Behind any one or all of these reasons a woman may have fallen into identification with the mother archetype, where maternity comprises life's sole value. Whatever a woman's motivation, a man involved with a woman obsessed with getting pregnant may well feel himself devoured, reduced to his semen-producing potential, no more than a magic stick, an object for a woman's aim, and thus reduced to a drone's servitude in fertilizing a queen.

In seeking the pregnancy to which she feels entitled, Tamar

puts on a veil to disguise herself as a prostitute. Translations differ in the exact wording of this point. Does Tamar disguise herself as a whore (*zona*), or is she a sacred prostitute (*qedesa*), a woman who dedicates herself to serving god or goddess through her sexuality?[11]

Sacred prostitution was widely practiced in Canaanite sanctuaries. A woman's veiling indicated dedication to the goddess Ishtar.[12] Every woman, at least once in her life, sat in the temple and received in the goddess's name a man who was a stranger to her who himself represented an incarnate god. Sexual congress, through sympathetic magic, assured fertility of the land, of the flocks, and of the family. One was thus infused with some of the divine force, sexuality as the act of creation. In this view, sexuality does not entirely belong to us; nor does it work solely to our ego purposes; we acknowledge it as also belonging to the non-ego and beyond-ego world. Here female equals blood, milk, body, fertility, and continuity of life. She is not yet an individual person, as Jesus was to see her, but primordial natural force, awesome in its power to bring life, to convey the transcendent through sexual ecstasy. In this sense her body is not just a vehicle but a presence, divine energy housed in the flesh. Through it she opens a man to the penetration of the divine and opens herself to the encompassing of it.[13] A primary offering to the ancient goddess was in this womanly welcoming of the stranger who might be a god in the flesh.[14] The mystery of the sexual meeting thus regenerates spiritual presence. A portion of divine love remains housed in the flesh of the participants, and so they can sacrifice ego desires, power ambitions, all earthly values, to a greater authority, to wisdom made present, carried by the instincts and the emotions moved to love without possessiveness. So it is that sexual desire can express the divine force of life.

In the perversions of the Judeo-Christian tradition this vision of the conjunction of the sexual and the spiritual too often has been buried under moralizing "shoulds" and "should nots," so that the joy and the sacred solemnity of giving oneself over to another have been lost for many of us. But somewhere in ourselves all of us know the power and the goodness of this sexual sharing of being. Isn't this what is buried in a fairy-tale love that quickens both our response and our defensive dismissal of that love as nothing but a fairy tale? When the simple gardener in "The Twelve Dancing Princesses" loves the youngest princess enough to follow her into the underworld and bring her back up into the everyday world, along with her sisters and their dancing, we rejoice in the reunion of fantasy and fact, of passion and enduring relationship.[15] When the heroine travels the forest, seas, and glass mountains in "East of the Wind and West of the Moon" to free her beloved from the wicked witch's spell, and does so with the great feat of laundering-out the staining spot, we laugh in delight at the way a silly task accomplishes a profound transformation of the male from mother's boy to a person potent in his own right.

What Tamar touches here is just such transformative feminine power to mix body and soul, flesh and spirit, to bring the divine into immediate touch with everyday human reality. This is what comes into Jesus' lineage with the alien female and her outlawed religious practices. Perhaps it is from this source in Tamar that Jesus' power comes to free woman from being nothing but a symbol for impersonal blood, milk, fertility, and sex, to let her emerge in her own person. Remembering Tamar, we remember the primordial power of woman's sexuality, and with her and with it the binding relationship of sexuality and spirituality in the line of the Saving One.

Many women do not achieve sexual ecstasy because they do not allow into full consciousness the great force of this spiritual level of their sexuality. It asks so much; it gives so much. It feels like meeting with a force that transcends our human powers. We are afraid of it, and religion, having so often been used to combat it, may have left some strong lingering doubts about it in us. It does, after all, reach well beyond a woman's personal relation with her partner at the same time as it infuses that relation with physical ecstasy. Can she really receive so strong a mixing of sexual and spiritual? The answer, I think, is clear: the human dimension makes it possible to survive the intensity of the divine by providing a container through which it can flow.

Too much religious teaching has acted to sever the links between the human and divine dimensions of our sexuality and thus contributed to a childishness that keeps blocking our sexual development. It is a psycholgical commonplace that when a man does not differentiate the feminine component of his own sexuality from its mother-container, his image of a woman cannot develop beyond the level we associate with the prostitute—a woman who exists to serve him.[16] Judah defines this demeaning categorization of woman and its constrictions. The dreams of some people of today show a way out of it, pointing to a knitting that may be possible, a reweaving of the connection between the human and the divine, the sexual and the spiritual.

Here are two such dreams, those of a woman in her fifties who identifies herself as Christian. The dreams occurred a month apart, but she felt they both addressed the same task. In the first she is in her childhood church. Her beloved husband is there, too, but in the background, not figuring in the dream events. She sees herself before the Eucharist service, in the passionate embrace of a priest figure, a man who is a stranger to her. Their mouths are joined; his penis penetrates her vagina. "This is unobstructed love and passion," she says. Then they part for the service of the Eucharist. Here, what our religion too often separates is brought together: the sexual embrace of the two opposites, male and female, paralleled in the mysterious communion of the divine and human in the Mass. Sex and spirit join. The dreamer felt her deep love for her husband made possible her embrace of the inner figure of the stranger. The psychic container of their personal relation enabled her to embrace the impersonal sexuality in her psyche. He was part of her own psyche. Her love for her husband and her living of it acted as container.[17]

The second dream took place by the sea, hence close to the waters of the unconscious. In it a faithful nun meets passionately with a lover, saying to him that she will "cape" him. This takes place right in a large baptismal font that in the dream is called a "ciborium." The dream surprised the dreamer. Again the mysterious combination within one woman of a faithful and virgin love of God with the ecstasy of intense sexual passion shows that one does not cancel the other but contains it. The virgin symbolized a chaste consciousness, one uncontaminated by man-made ambitions, deviousness, and standards and tough enough to relate to "transpersonal energies without identifying with them."[18] The dreamer said that to "cape" meant to cover the man's phallus with her genitals. The baptismal font meant rebirth; it marked a belonging to the family of God, not just to a family of human origin. The woman did not know what a ciborium was and had to look it up in the dictionary. To her amazement it was defined as a canopied (i.e., a caped) shrine, a receptacle for the reservation of the Eucharist. Thus one word, "cape," linked all these things— intimate sexual exchange, rebirth into the knowledge that we belong to God and the people of God, and a mysterious mingling of human and divine elements at the most sacred moment of a religious service. The sexual and spiritual both act in the dream as rites of renewal of the human through the taking in of the divine.[19]

When Judah approaches Tamar at the gate, Tamar lets him believe what he wants. Many different forms of sexual trickery and denial combine in her, initiating the trickster motif that repeats itself with Rahab and with Ruth.[20] Judah tries to trick Tamar by temporizing about fulfilling his obligation to provide her with a husband to secure offspring. He tries to set her aside, to leave her as a father's daughter, rather than a woman recognized in her own right.

With daring, Tamar, unloved and pushed aside, takes the initiative to bring about what she knows as right in Israel's law. She herself sets aside conventions imposed by society in general, by men in particular, in order to arrive at her truth that will be Yahweh's truth. She knows what she is doing in tricking Judah, whereas Judah at the gate is acting without knowledge. He is moved by simple sexual passion, not, at least as he understands events, by passion for Israel. Tamar's self-possession and assertiveness to secure an heir lead her to trickery and disguise in order to undo Judah's trickery, denial, and deceit.[21] His trickery fails, just as his initial judgment of her falls to the ground before his own guilt. Her trickery succeeds when she shows him his own identifying emblems, demonstrating that he, not she, cast her as the harlot. Some commentators think Judah was allowed to be tricked to punish him for selling his brother Joseph to the Egyptians. Tamar, however, by any interpretation, cannot be said to be tricked. She moves with conscious strength to achieve her place in the Tree of Jesse. She can rely on her own wits to protect her rights, and she, of all people, ends up mitigating Judah's guilt by bearing an ancestor of David. Thus Tamar takes on tones of one who, like a Job, mediates for others after her own severe testing and travail.

Tamar is a figure of disorder and counterorder. Through

elements that are alien and expressly excluded and condemned in the scriptural world, Tamar effects a new order and moves it toward its exalted end in Jesus. Not only does she bring with her the great, distant, frightening, and mysterious motifs of the *vagina dentata* and sacred prostitution, but her trickery succeeds through an incestuous coupling of a daughter and a father-in-law. This incestuous act is not only conscious, but owned and claimed publicly. Unlike actual abusive incest or obsessive incest fantasies, which serve the regressive purpose of keeping a daughter under a father's control, this intentional act leads Tamar out of her father's house to establish not just a house of her own, but one of eternal significance in the future of Israel. Once again a stone that builders have rejected becomes a cornerstone. Tamar—feared, denied, and set aside— is such a cornerstone upon whom the edifice of the Messiah is to be built.

THREE

RAHAB

RAHAB'S STORY IS told in Joshua (2:1–24). It is the time of Israel's entry into the promised land after forty years of wandering in the desert and the conquering of the city-state of Jericho. We have heard many sermons—and songs—about Joshua and the battle of Jericho. But do we know about the help of Rahab that made that battle and its outcome possible? It is an astonishing story, of the largest religious and psychological significance.

Joshua sends two men to map the territory of the Canaanite king of Jericho. They lodge with the harlot Rahab in a house near the gate of the town wall. When the spies are reported to the authorities, a search begins that eventually reaches Rahab's house. She hides the spies under flax drying on her roof, explaining that Joshua's men have left and moved off far away from where they are being sought. Then she makes her terms with the spies: "I know the Lord has given you the land . . . ," she says. "For we have heard how the Lord dried up the water of the Red Sea before you when you came out of Egypt, and what you did to the two kings . . . whom you utterly destroyed. . . . Our hearts melted, . . . no courage left in any man, because of you." Your God, she says to them, "is God in heaven above, and in earth beneath."

She proposes a deal. Save me, she says, and all my family—father, mother, sisters, brothers, and their families—as I have saved you. The spies agree. They instruct Rahab to tie a scarlet thread to her window, the same color as the cord she has used to get them down through her window to make their escape. The deal is struck. She should bring all her relatives to her house, but no one must go out. When Joshua attacks, his army will spare Rahab's house, clearly identified by the red thread, and all inside it. That is what happens. When Jericho falls, Rahab and her family alone survive to become citizens of Israel and believers in its religion.

Once again, we see one of Jesus' female ancestors rising from a foreign land, king, and culture. Like Tamar, Rahab is alien. She is a Canaanite, subject of a kingdom that is no more than a conglomeration of city-states, located in a circumscribed area. As a harlot, Rahab is a foreigner in her own country, her profession putting her well outside the bounds of respectable citizens. Unlike Tamar, who is linked to sacred prostitution and religious rite, Rahab is a working girl of the streets, the most prosaic example of a whore. But she is well placed for her role; people come in and out of her house at the gate as she does her business, and so she hears and sees things from the near and far sides of her society. Mostly, she is a woman distanced from centers, from her own society and from Israel's, from religious orthodoxy, like all these female ancestors. They are women set aside, bits of another world, off-center, and yet, in their place in the Tree of Jesse—like Rahab's position at the gate—they are right in the main line of sacred history.

Like Tamar, Rahab indulges in trickery to reach her goal, knowing she can depend on no one but herself. Unlike Tamar, who is forced to use tricks, Rahab lies and deceives deliberately—turning tricks is her profession, after all—and moves to save herself and others with the great trick of the red cord. Red, as "the zenith of the colors," symbolizes the sun and all war gods; it represents the active masculine principle. It is fire, passion, blood, as well as ardor, ferocity, energy, and sexual excitement. It can mean life, love, and warmth, as well as anger, vengeance, hellfire. In Christian tradition, red stands for Christ's blood shed at Calvary; it blazons the zeal of faith, the fire of Pentecost, martyrdom.[1]

Rahab shows this mode of active masculinity in the sense of knowing what she wants and going right to it. Nowhere in her story do we read of her showing hesitation or ambivalence or regret for her actions. She sets her course and accomplishes its consummation. In this sense, she can be seen as a woman who harnesses her power to get and to do, to establish her purpose and achieve it, to focus upon her goal and eschew any distractions that might arise through competing feelings or tenderhearted regrets over the fact that life can be so hard. Like a soldier or warrior herself, she can be understood as a woman who has masculine energies at her disposal and is not afraid to use them.[2]

On one level Rahab is simply out for herself. She looks at two warring sides, concludes that hers has no chance of victory, and aligns herself with the winner. But at another level, she is moved to go well beyond herself, both terrified and awed by the power of the God of Israel, who has stopped the sea and defeated kings for his people.

Precisely these opposites—tough self-reliance and vulnerability to the unseen and imagined—show in the case of a young woman, working as a prostitute, who came to seek therapy. She combined the realism of frank assessment of which men would be the best "tricks" with a capacity for lavish response—unmeasured, outpouring—for her family. These are the same opposing qualities that meet in Rahab. She goes right to the point of things, looking to see who will win and where her safety lies. She recognizes the majesty of Israel's God and willingly gives herself over to it: "The Lord your God really *is* God, both in heaven and on earth below."

Rahab thus instructs us in the ways of grace. If we take the grace offered to us, we will find that it benefits many others around us. Rahab knows how to save her family in their great number (it has been reckoned that there were two hundred of her kinfolk).[3] She intercedes for her family as its self-appointed savior, just as Tamar's action redeems Judah's failure to fulfill the law by providing her with a husband and hence with offspring. Grace results in such intercession. Grace is never a private possession, but is contagious, epidemic in its effects. It cannot be confined, but inexorably moves through one person to another and to another and another.[4]

When grace is offered, we take it or face losing it altogether. When we confront the Holy, the All in All, which is unconditioned in its wholeness, we are given the chance to respond in wholeness with nothing held back. Rahab shows us how in doing so we will even betray if necessary, strike deals, use every kind of trick. We go with it wholeheartedly and do not miss our chances. For the sake of the God she has glimpsed, Rahab determines to hold fast to grace and break all other ties. Her highest loyalty now is to God. She has been totally reorganized—except in her skills as a trickster. Isn't she then an example of faithful response to the First Commandment, loving God with all her heart, and mind, and soul and strength?

Such zeal and determination, such dedicated trickery, are foreign and alien elements in our contemporary religion. We prefer to avoid speaking about such things or even noticing that they exist. This is a tough world, coarsely commercial, like a whore's contract. Here is what is offered. We take it and we pay for it. Or leave it, forget it. Rahab perceives Yahweh's might and truth and completely gives herself and all of her large family over to his keeping. She sees. She acts. In theological language, we say that she corresponds with grace.[5]

This is the rough side of grace, what used to be called "God's wrath." It is the other side of the coin: we either receive grace or live outside it, which is to say, in God's wrath, among the damned, with those who refuse what God offers. Sometimes, when grace comes, there is no time to sharpen our pencils, get paper out to list the pluses and minuses of God's offering. Take it, or leave it and be left. Rahab measured up to this confrontation. She knew what she had seen.

Most of us dread this aspect of grace. To take it can feel like a leap into the abyss. We remember all those examples of horrible acts done to people in the name of that higher loyalty to God that abrogates all lesser ties. We think of terrorists blowing up airports in the name of God. We think of those clamorous people who come into school or city government or church with their mission, to guide us in more violent ways. We think of the parents in fringe religions who say it is their holy responsibility to save their child from perdition, from the depradations of medicine, for example. We run from such a faith. We flee such madness. God save us from such destructive self-righteous religion! And yet central to faith, no matter how little it is acknowledged, is this direct taking or leaving, this corresponding to or refusing grace. How can we tell the difference between a grace that is true and the fanatical distortion of grace?

The worst thing to say is that we cannot finally, clearly, with any guarantee of safety, make the distinction, tell the difference between a true offering of grace and the appropriation of its manner as pretext for coercion and destruction. We point instead to one sure test that proceeds from the Second Commandment. Will this grace result in our loving our neighbor, or will it make us more angry, pushy, moody, petty,

mean-spirited, violent in our anger? That is a rule used in the
New Testament, used again by Teresa of Avila, used by Jung.[6]

But what about Rahab? Though good to the spies sent by
Joshua and the incoming troops, she is a traitor to her city and
king. Though good to her large family, she betrays the rest of
the people in her country. How, from such an example, can
we tell when to answer grace's offer with our whole heart, and
when to be cautious, or just to turn away?

Let us look at what Rahab really did. The *Midrash Rabbah*
says she clove to Israel and accepted Torah. Israel became her
people, her country, her faith.[7] The rabbis spun around her a
priestly association through her use of flax to hide the spies on
her roof. From such flax came the fine linen that priests wore
to perform their religious duties. The rabbis reckon ten priest-
prophets as "descended from Rahab the harlot." They also associate with her all of the families that wrought fine linen for
David, who busied himself with the curtain of the Ark and the
tent of the Holy of Holies.[8]

The spinning of fabric is a major symbol associated with the
feminine mode of being. Spinning is symbolically equivalent
to bringing forth being, that most feminine act, that crucial
enactment of being.

The spindle, so central in spinning, connects Jesus' ancestor
Rahab with the feminine deities for whom the spindle is a major identifying attribute. This includes "all the Mother Goddesses, the lunar goddesses and weavers of fate in their terrible
aspect."[9] The spinners offer a different trinity from the accus-
tomed one of Father, Son, and Spirit in Christian tradition, a
female trinity that spins into human fabric birth, life, and
death, or past, present, and future. The two elements usually
considered good, birth and life, are met by the third, usually
considered evil or cruel, death, which breaks the thread of life.
The spindle in its turning motion symbolizes "unchanging

lawfulness, inexorable fate, or eternal return."[10] It represents both the transitoriness of life and the *Magna Mater* spinning at the top of the Tree of Life, emblem of the intersection of heaven and earth and the sacrifice that renews the generating force of the universe.[11] Spinning and weaving "represent the feminine principle in its skills of weaving destiny and the veil of the world of illusion."[12]

Here, in trying to understand how to correspond with grace, we must act like the rabbis, amplifying the imagery that Scripture gives us, reading the way they do, allegorically, not literally. We must spin and spin about spinning, and see spinning as similar to weaving, as associated with the Virgin at her loom in, say, Byzantine iconography.

Spinning of Rahab's kind has to do with fine linen, not work shirts but garments reserved for the religious mysteries. What does this mean psychologically? What it does is take the psychological process of association to a new and highly differentiated level, where we can meditate on religious truths and allow to spin around them in full consciousness the complex clusters of thoughts, feelings, and images that they may evoke. The chaff must be weeded out, the thread made fine and delicate and yet strong. Thus will evil in the form of base thought fall to the ground, and feeble imaginings, evil's collaborators, be excluded. What is bestowed by this kind of spinning is a subtlety of attitude that excludes coarse equations. No more "this equals that" or "this is nothing but. . . ."[13] In such fineness of spirit, as with the fine linen of Scripture, we penetrate to the core of things, touch the actuality of a situation as it is lived. Nothing is reduced to simplistic rules or regulations that legislate the letter and miss the spirit of the law.

Let us think here of our attempts to pray and meditate, to engage in a spiritual life, and think of our worship together. When we enter prayer with a spinning attitude prayer works;

an atmosphere of possibility is generated. We speak to God and hear God speaking to us through a circulation of insights and feelings that well up in us, new images that live in us, clear answers that seem to be spoken to us. When we lack a spinning attitude prayer does not work; we frown over a Bible passage, struggle to reach a prescribed stage in prayer, enforce on ourselves the received rules, how we ought to do it. How boring to do; how boring to hear! Nothing happens; and we cannot even lean into the nothingness to feel the presence of the Other who is there, pulling the props from under us. We just feel put aside, neglected, unsupported, even though we know the rules, know with certainty what should happen next.[14]

In worship, when this attitude of spinning is missing, we plod through the liturgy but feel no presence, not our own, not others', certainly not God's. The service is crude because it follows set designs without any quickening life. But spinning as an attitude of worship takes us far from the deadening, empowers us with a subtlety and fullness of reception that sees the unseen in the seen. We perceive a lasting quality in the barest facts that proclaim God's presence in the everyday work of praying and worshiping. Our feeling about what happens goes beyond the general collective reaction. The general is eclipsed in the special, the abstract in the concrete. When we confess, for example, we are not just reciting words but connecting to specific obstacles to grace such as holding grudges, or insisting on our own way no matter what, or refusing to see some part of the other or others in our life. With the spinning attitude we create a delicate and tough consciousness through which we can see the concrete tangible issues confronting us and the fullness of others that surround us.

Fine linen is spun to be made into specific robes for officiating priests, or specific fabrics for the curtains of the Ark of the Covenant. The cloths cover everything, but guarantee nothing. In the spinning attitude we know for a fact that we cannot have rules for prayer that make it work every time, or rubrics for worship that certify a sense of God's presence at regular repeatable intervals. The spinning attitude means recognizing each meeting with the Holy as a special case, unique to itself. What will happen this time? What quality of meeting will arrive with this prayer? The time and the meeting will bring their own unpredictable answers.

One of the occupational hazards for the clergy is the danger of droning on in rote recital of a liturgy, preoccupied with the mechanics of posture, position, and pace, failing to spin that exquisite attention necessary to approach the Holy of Holies. If the priest is not worshiping as she or he conducts a service, the spinning attitude will be withheld from the congregation. We may be doing the right thing, but for the wrong situation, unlike Rahab, who does the wrong thing, acting the traitor, which is exactly right for her situation.

Doing the right thing in a merely general, collective way deadens instead of quickens. If the spinning is not fresh on each occasion in relation to the Holy, the chances are we will not connect with anything, including ourselves. In teaching, for example, if the teacher is not learning something at every class, then chances are the students are not learning anything in a real, life-changing way either. Even if the class looks good, follows the rules precisely, sounds spirited and warm, if it lacks that true weaving back and forth between student, teacher, and material, it must miss. It has lost its living particularity in a deadening general service. A true weaving brings all of us into the central life of the Trinity, right there on the second floor of a school building, on a hot September night, with traffic noises howling outside the windows.

We might well ask how the Trinity can live in an ordinary classroom. We experience it through the interchange, the fine weavings, between the students—with all their insights, questions, hopes, problems, and arguments; the teacher—with all his or her training, authority gained through decades of work, questions, hopes, problems, and arguments; and the material—with its wealth of content, allusion, questioning, raising of problems and arguments in support of its version of the truth. Those three sets of living elements engage in conversation, and a weaving and spinning gets going of such intensity that new things happen rising neither from the students, nor the teacher, nor the material, but through some presence that becomes palpable through the interchanges among the three. New ideas happen to the teacher, things never thought or felt before. The same happens to the students, and the material itself also seems to unfold as never before at new depths, pointing beyond itself with a new clarity of direction. The atmosphere crackles with excitement, not unlike the rushing wind or fire associated with the Pentecost.

Rahab, like Tamar, is a woman so far from deadening rote that she is able to choose at the moment a whole new life that is suddenly unexpectedly offered her. She is so wholly alive in her new-found faith that in spite of her profession we can speak of the virginal quality of being in her, not defined by her relation to others, but by her seeing through to the truth others bring with them.[15] For Tamar, the virginizing renewal is found in the necessity she feels to conceive a child and go well out of herself in so doing. For Rahab, it is in her desire to give herself utterly to Yahweh. These women become virgins again, not physically but spiritually. They cannot be defined by general laws. They break such rules in order to abide by them, Tamar by making Judah impregnate her, Rahab by betraying as the way to be faithful to God. Unfettered by convention or their own ego-values, such women sacrifice everything to the larger Self that God can bring about through them. Tamar bears the ancestor of David in the tribe of Judah. Rahab, it is reasonably assumed, becomes the wife of Salmon and mother of Boaz, ancestor of David, and thus a direct part of Jesus' line.[16]

The linking of Rahab—as one altogether contained in herself, even though that causes her to break rules in order to sustain them—with the motif of spiritual and psychological virginity brings us to the final religious truth that she serves. She is an incomparable example of how the last shall be first. Rahab is definitively of the last, a whore cast aside, living in a house at the city gate, with a rabble of sexual users coming in and out, unprotected by husband, father, or brother. And yet it is she who becomes her family's intercessor, she who is shown to be first in faith, marked as such in Hebrews and James. In the letter to the Hebrews, she is hailed as one of the great examples of obedience—she, the trickster and traitor: "By faith the harlot Rahab did not perish with those who were disobedient . . ." (11:31a). For James, she is an example of those who are justified by their works—she, the master of the works we should properly call dirty tricks: "You see that a man is justified by works and not by faith alone. And in the same way was not also Rahab the harlot justified by works when she received the messengers and sent them out another way?" (2:24–25). Thus in Rahab is the Reformation quarrel between Catholic and Protestant resolved, for Rahab is justified both by her faith and her works.

There is more. Rahab brings home to us the fact of faith, that the greatest faith and most moving works demonstrate that none of us is deserving or could be. It is God who gives victory over Jericho. It is God's loving-kindness and faithfulness (*chesed* and *emeth*) with which the spies, speaking for God, say they will deal with her.[17] Thus she is given and thus she gives herself into the special keeping of God. She is neither righteous nor deserving, any more than Israel is nor any one of us.

We do not earn God's love and protection; God gives it to us, well beyond our merits, and we receive it, quickly, thankfully, all the more because we know how little we deserve it. That is what Rahab teaches us, as Jesus does. We know in our hearts—and if we do not know it, our enemies will tell us; hence one good reason for the injunction to love our enemies—how often we have turned away from God, how often we fall into the terrible sin of refusal. Rahab—whore, liar, traitor—is a true Christ-figure. She shows us that it is God who acts, beyond us, for us, in us, and that when we respond as we should respond, we become blessed.

FOUR

RUTH

RUTH IS THE BEST known of the ancestresses of Jesus, and her story has become a fable for all, religious and nonreligious. In the time of the rule of the Judges over Israel, the land of Judah, the family of Elimelech, Naomi, and their two sons, Mahlon and Chilion, leaves Bethlehem to settle in Moab. Elimelech dies there, and his two sons settle down and marry two Moabite women, Orpah and Ruth. After ten years, the sons too die. Naomi, their mother, hears that life has improved in Bethlehem and decides to return to her own people. She implores her daughters-in-law to return to their own mothers in the hope of finding husbands again. They do not want to leave her, but Naomi says she is too old to give them more sons. She has nothing herself, no hope for a husband; the Lord's hand has gone out against her. They weep together, and Orpah decides to return to her mother. But Ruth remains, clinging to Naomi, speaking the familiar words: "Entreat me not to leave thee, or to return from following after thee: for whither thou goest I will go; and where thou lodgest, I will lodge: thy people shall be my people, and thy God my God. Where thou diest, will I die, and there will I be buried: the Lord do so to me, and more also, if ought but death part thee and me" (Ruth 1:16–17).

The two women return to Bethlehem, where Naomi says to the women who greet her (like a hum of bees, says one commentor[1]): "Call me not Naomi; call me Mara: for the Almighty hath dealt bitterly with me. I went out full, and the Lord brought me home again empty" (Ruth 1:20–21). Naomi refers to leaving with two sons and a husband and returning with none of them, for they are all dead.

Naomi and Ruth really have nothing, no home, no food, no future, only faith in Yahweh to support them. Ruth decides to work in the barley field of Boaz, a wealthy kinsman of Naomi's husband. She impresses Boaz, who takes her under his protection as one of his maidservants in the field and allows her to eat and draw water, warning the young men around her not to molest her. He makes sure each day that she goes home with food. He does this, he says, because of the kindness she has shown her mother-in-law. Boaz prays, he tells her, that "a full reward be given thee of the Lord God of Israel, under whose wing thou art come to trust" (Ruth 2:12).

Sometime later Boaz celebrates with his men the end of the barley harvest, planning to sleep that night at the threshing floor. Naomi tells Ruth to put on her best clothes and to wait until after the celebration, after Boaz has gone to sleep; then, in the dead of night, she instructs her, she is to lie down at Boaz's feet, uncover the lower part of his body, and wait for him to tell her what to do. Ruth does all of this. Boaz awakes, startled at feeling a woman near him. Who is it? he asks. Ruth identifies herself and asks him to bless her by spreading his wings over her and by pulling the skirt of his garment over her. Boaz says he will do so because of her kindness, this last even greater than her first, seeking him out rather than going after younger men. Boaz soon agrees to marry Ruth and to redeem the land of Naomi's kinsman. He bids her stay with him till morning and then leave before others can see her, sending her home with measures of barley heaped in the veil she uses to cover herself.

At the city gates, Boaz asks a nearer kinsman of Naomi if he wants to redeem the bit of land that belongs to her. He does, but when Boaz adds that Ruth comes with the land, so that she may produce an heir to whom the land would revert, the kinsman backs away. Boaz then claims both land and Ruth, retaining the name of her late husband. Those who hear this call down blessings upon Boaz and Ruth, among them the significant words, "May your house be like the house of Perez, whom Tamar bore Judah, because of the children that the Lord will give you by this young woman" (Ruth 4:12).

Ruth bears a son for Boaz, whom they name Obed. He, in a direct line, will father Jesse, who will father David. The crucial ancestry is established. The women bless Naomi and say it is Ruth, even more than her son, who is the boon: "He shall be to you a restorer of life and nourisher of your old age; for your daughter-in-law who loves you, who is more to you than seven sons, has borne him" (Ruth 4:15).

Moab is east of the Dead Sea. Like Tamar and Rahab in their generations, Ruth comes from Moab as a foreigner to Israel. In the words of one commentator, she demonstrates that "an essential dimension of Israel is the foreign feminine east" whence Abraham also came. [2]

The Moabites descend from Lot. They represent a distinctly different path from Abraham's and from the law of Israel. Lot and Abraham, we will remember, journeyed westward together and then parted ways, Lot returning eastward to the city of Sodom. He went back in the direction from where he had come. Psychologically, we might see this as symbolizing regression, a return to a previous standpoint. Religiously, the previous place represented a polytheistic, matriarchal, goddess culture. When Sodom was doomed, Lot, his wife, and two daughters were rescued through Abraham's intervention, suggesting a continuing connection between the new religion of Israel and its matriarchal forebears. This family of four suggests the symbolism of the quaternity, of wholeness. But it is lopsided, composed of three women to one man, and it breaks down because Lot's wife looked back and was turned into a pillar of salt; that is, unlike her husband, she yearned to remain with her previous religion and is arrested there, fixed in place. Salt symbolizes both bitterness and wisdom, but here there is too much salt, not the few grains that add savor or proportion to things. Unable to move forward to a new, enlarging vision, Lot's wife is caught in bitterness. Her husband and two daughters journey on and settle down in a cave, where the daughters make their father drunk and then lie with him. From the first to give birth comes Moab. Thus we can associate Ruth with a place where the feminine quite overpowers the masculine. The mother is lost, unable to develop further. But still the father retreats into the maternal, to the womb, in the form of a cave, and retreats even further into drunken unconsciousness, and his daughters overpower him in incest.

This dominance of the feminine over the masculine stands in sharp contrast to the beginning of Ruth's story. There, in the land of Judah, under Yahweh's law, famine has erupted, an act of God symbolizing deep disturbance in the religious and psychological atmosphere. It is an unfruitful world; it does not support life. In this family of four, of Naomi, her husband and two sons, the quaternity is also lopsided, now the masculine outweighing the feminine. This family leaves the country of patriarchal religion to go back to the country of matriarchal religion to get food. But the father, whose name, Elimelech, means "My God (Yahweh) is king," dies, suggesting that the predominant masculine emphasis must end. Later, the two sons, Mahlon (from the root that means *holeh*, "sick") and Chi-

lion (from several roots meaning "coming to an end"), also die.[3]
The three men who start out with just one woman, forming a
most lopsided quaternity, are quickly dead, and the women—
Naomi and her daughters-in-law Ruth and Orpah—are now at
the center of things. But this new grouping does not work either. We need the right mixture of feminine and masculine.
Monotheistic Yahwist faith sees itself as an advance over the
polytheistic nature religion of Moab. To return to Moab for
food in time of famine is one thing. To return to settle there
permanently is like a psychological regression to a previous
state of consciousness. We know from depth psychology that
once we reach a new point of consciousness, we cannot go back
to a previous stage. It will not work. It is a false unconsciousness, like an attempt to deny something we already know.[4]

Naomi's journey to Moab is better seen as a necessary regression in the service of the ego, looking to reconnect with
something valuable that was left behind or was lost in the religion of Israel. This surely has to do with the feminine config-
urations of religion, because that is what the Old Testament
associates to Moab, though in disapproving terms (see Num.
5:1, ". . . the people began to commit harlotry with the daughters of Moab"). (See also Num. 22:3–6, where the Moabites
call on Balaam to curse the Hebrews.)

Moab, then, is the country of the goddesses' religion, as-
serted in a licentiousness of sexual passion, in a bounty of nature that feeds human life, and in a death-bringing
countermasculinity for the three men who die there. In the
background of the book of Ruth, we can feel the mythological
motif of a dying and rising god. Naomi loses her husband and
sons and becomes nurse to the newly born restorer of the clan;
Ruth moves from loss and destitution through harvest to
bounty as wife and mother. The husbands and sons, who are
overpowered by the all-feminine Moab religion, come to life

again in the combination of the feminine with the masculine Hebrew faith, in Boaz marrying Ruth and producing the newborn Obed.[5]

Ruth brings with her into her new Hebrew faith that alien element of counterorder that her sister ancestresses brought before her. But where with Tamar it was the counterorder of sacred prostitution in the service of the house of Judah and the line of David and Jesus, and with Rahab the counterorder of treason in the service of faith, with Ruth it is the counterorder of an initiating female in a man's world. Ruth, much more than the other ancestresses, is herself a Christ figure. In Ruth, Israel recovers its origins from the East, which is to say from "its own otherness."[6]

Like Abraham, who also came from the East, Ruth leaves the familiar for the alien. She journeys from the East to a land and people she does not know. In this way she prefigures Jesus' saying, "If any one comes to me and does not hate his own father and mother and wife and children and brothers and sisters, yes, and even his own life, he cannot be my disciple" (Luke 14:26). Ruth leaves everything she has known but, unlike Abraham, without the comfort of divine call or promise. She has only the love and loyalty she feels for another woman to sustain her. Ruth is no patriarch; she is only a single woman, a widow, who must argue, even with her mother-in-law, about her determination to follow her to Bethlehem. She is a heroic figure, journeying from the security of her mother's house to a strange land and people where she has no home.[7] But she will not go back, will not regress to being simply a mother's daughter, as Naomi proposes to her, bidding her to return to her mother's house. Nor will she wait for a man to validate her. She willingly gives up her chance for a future marriage and security in her own country for insecurity in Judah. She brings with her from the foreign East the counterorder of a woman's courage to make her way in a man's world, out of love for another woman.[8] Thus she plants a new seed in Israel's history, one that reveals another side of Yahweh's love, a fierce and yet tender feminine side that shelters the faithful, even the alien faithful.

In Ruth, some commentators think, the text pleads for the inclusion of foreigners in Israel, counteracting a narrow nationalism.[9] In the New Testament, Peter enunciates this view when he says that God is no respecter of persons and will show no partiality, for anyone who fears God and does what is right will be found acceptable (Acts 10:35).

In addition to introducing her alien ancestry as the founding source of David's and Jesus' line, Ruth asserts a precious element foreign to patriarchal culture, that of the initiating woman who makes things happen. Ruth acts as subject in her story, not as an object to be disposed of by men.[10] No one steps forward to help Naomi—or herself—until Ruth acts, working out not only their own salvation this way but ours, in securing the great line from David to Jesus.

In going with Naomi, Ruth forsakes tribal clan and religion. And this despite Naomi's repeated urging that Ruth and Orpah each return to her mother's house in a society that is clearly matriarchal. This is not because Ruth had no father, for we learn in 2:11 that she has left both mother and father. Naomi here represents the feminine as it will be included in the patriarchal Hebrew faith, in contrast to the religion of the land of Moab, where the matriarchal nature goddess, with her endless cycles of dying and rising vegetation, holds sway. Naomi disidentifies herself from this "nature-mother" because the Lord, who has remembered his people, now gives them bread; that is, she seeks the inclusion of the feminine in the life-giving Hebrew faith where a spiritual God reigns.[11] Naomi does not return to Israel without grief, however. She mourns for her daughters-in-law; when she returns to Bethlehem she complains that God has dealt "bitterly" with her, has "afflicted" her, has brought her back "empty," despite the fact that Ruth accompanies her. Thus Naomi does not recognize in a patriarchal setting the full value of the feminine.

Naomi is now barren, her sons and husband dead. Her complaint points to the suffering of women as a major shift occurs in the creative principle as configured in nature religions and in the Yahwist faith. In nature religions the creative principle is found in the earth, in the body, nature, sexuality, the female. The male is a necessary but subsidiary fructifying phallus in service to the female, who brings forth new life. In the Hebrew faith, the creative principle lodges in the fiat, word, and command of Yahweh alone. Creation comes through the spirit, not the body. This text and others, as Kluger points out, say that the initial effect of this shift on women is deeply disturbing—it represents barrenness: Sarah conceives only after she has submitted to God's messengers (Gen. 18:9–15); Hannah conceives only after she has dedicated her son to God (1 Sam. 1:9–11).[12] Naomi feels barren, greatly saddened at having to send away her daughters, who symbolize the polytheistic goddess religion of Moab. Orpah does as she is told and disappears from the story. Some legends say she was punished for her refusal to follow Naomi all the way into Hebrew faith.[13] Orpah, in these tales, later gives birth to four giants, who mark the four miles of her journey with Naomi. Goliath was one of these giants, killed by Ruth's descendant, David, in the course of his conquering of Philistine territory for Yahweh.

Ruth, quite differently, comes with full heart and feeling into her new Yahwist faith, consciously choosing this religious devotion through her personal devotion to Naomi, thus healing the older woman's bitterness with her own young love. This suggests that the feminine that Naomi represents—a feminine

wounded by patriarchy, and made bitter and barren—is redeemed by the feminine that Ruth represents—a feminine
fully open, all the way down to its passionate earthy roots, and
all the way up through personal love for another woman to the
most devoted feeling for the spirit represented by Naomi's
God. This is the conscious feminine, the full-bodied, full-spir-
ited feminine. Like Tamar, but with a more advanced accent,
Ruth joins sex and spirit, not just to maternity but to a flow-
ering of spirituality and sexuality with maternity, in that order
of precedence. Furthermore, Ruth reaches this fulfillment
through a most feminine means—identification with another
woman. She exemplifies the feminine mode of being here,
where to do for another is to be for them, to be one with
them.[14] Ruth brings into patriarchy a new feminine capacity
that is durable, tough, and tender, a love for the feminine in
concrete attachment between women that gives itself to God.

Ruth and Naomi now concoct schemes to follow their devotion where it leads.[15] Ruth secures protection in Boaz's field,
where he treats her, a stranger, as one of his own maidservants. By chance, the text says, Ruth gleans in the field of
Boaz, the kin of Elimelech. But the reader feels the working of
Divine Providence in the meeting. Ruth humbly asks permis-
sion to glean and then does so diligently. Boaz responds with
more fervor than we might expect even of a kindly landowner.
He tells her to glean only in his field, to keep with his maidservants, to come to eat with him; and he cautions his men
against molesting her and sends her home with food for Naomi. Ruth then falls on her face, bowed to the ground before
Boaz, asking why he should take notice of her, a foreigner.
Boaz answers that it is because of her loving service to Naomi;
he wants the Lord to give her complete reward. It is as if both
Boaz and Ruth felt a need to connect with each other, to give
special consideration to the "needy feminine."[16] When Ruth

returns to Naomi, she learns that Boaz is in fact kin and hence in a position to redeem them. What Boaz will do willingly for Ruth is precisely what Judah tried to avoid doing for Tamar, the duty of the levirate marriage. Not only will Boaz redeem the line of Elimelech but, in rescuing one family tree from extinction, he will uphold the whole corporate nature of Israel. The person is part of the family, the family part of the tribe, the tribe part of the people, and all belong to God. Breach of continuity disturbs the whole group and the group's wholeness. This is strongly underlined in the Book of Ruth, where restoration of the line of Elimelech through the foreign and female Ruth sustains continuity for the saving figure of David, and through David to Christ as savior.

Naomi takes the initiative and exerts a forthright purpose—to redeem her family—through wily feminine scheming.[17] Ruth and Naomi between them take a daring, even an outrageous, gamble, which brings Ruth to lie with Boaz at the threshing floor. And they win. Ruth secures her own and Naomi's future, so that she is compared with seven sons and declared greater than any of them.

Like Tamar and Rahab before her, Ruth is a trickster. She veils herself to hide in the night. The text itself veils her, for all we read is Naomi's instruction to uncover Boaz in the covering of her veil. The darkness then covers what happens next between them. We are left to imagine a sexual meeting that inspires Boaz's gratitude and firm resolve to make Ruth his wife. One of the Targum scholars makes a hilarious comment: when Boaz "bent forward and he beheld a woman at his feet," his "flesh became weak like a turnip."[18]

Ruth joins Tamar and Rahab in their psychological and spiritual virginity in the land of Israel. Commentators note her use of the veil, which also figures in the story of Tamar, and wonder if she is disguising herself as a sacred prostitute. The barley harvest is associated with fertility rites in the goddess cults, and Boaz's thrusting his gift of barley into her veil at the threshing floor could be seen as a survival of the custom of the hire of the hierodule at the fertility shrine, as well as a betrothal gift to Naomi for Ruth's hand. Moab was home to a chthonic deity, Chemosh, symbol of the underworld, and we feel in this story a contrast between that netherworld and Bethlehem, literally the house of bread and food.[19]

Some scholars even interpret the Book of Ruth as a fertility-cult narrative or as a Hebrew version of the Eleusis myth that focuses upon the interchange between mother and daughter and on the birth of a divine child.[20] Naomi and Ruth are a mother-daughter couple, not unlike the mythic Demeter-Kore figures. Through the symbolism of grain the two stories are linked. Demeter is the goddess of grain, and the ear of corn from which a child is born is a central symbol in the Eleusinian mysteries. Naomi instructs Ruth to wait upon Boaz at the threshing floor, and from this meeting at the grange a child will be conceived and born. Demeter and Kore are two aspects of the feminine, mother and daughter, hardly distinguishable from each other in terms of which one bears the child. When Ruth bears her child, the women exclaim, "There is a son born to Naomi" (4:17), thus underlining her identification with Ruth. In a way, we can see Ruth's adventures as redeeming the repressed femininity that Naomi may be understood to symbolize. But most scholars are uneasy with that imposition on the text of a preformed schema.

It is no imposition to insist on Ruth's virginal textures, both spiritual and psychological. Ruth's allegiance to Naomi and to Naomi's God is unremitting and pure, though Ruth has received no call from outside herself, has been given no theophany to direct her. Her devoted journey to a strange land and another people's God comes from the God present in her own

depths. With fierce dedication, Ruth knows to whom she belongs and what is good and right. She is intact psychologically
and spiritually. She cannot be sullied, misused, or entered by
man-made laws and customs.[21]

Ruth is uncannily like one of the nineteenth-century novelist
Trollope's heroines who go against family wishes and social
class divisions to stay true to their love for unlikely suitors.[22]
Her love comes to her all at once, whole; it grows secretly inside her, its details to be revealed slowly, bit by bit. It is a love
given to her rather than created by her. New to it, virginal,
she opens herself to it, consenting fully, which gives her the
strength to stay obdurate against all appeals of family, class,
custom, or self-preservation.

The *Midrash Rabbah* interprets Ruth's determination to go
with Naomi as a desire to be converted to Israel under any
circumstances and to destroy all idolatry within herself.[23] She
is in the deepest sense chaste, which means to put first things
first and lay aside all competing claims. No obstacles can inter-
fere with the primary and central loyalty that compels Ruth to
sacrifice one mother, one home country, one religion for another. The values of personal security and ego assertion, important as they are, yield in Ruth's faithfulness to the larger
reality of the divine. The collective ego values—roots, kinship,
and cultural reality—must be sacrificed so that Ruth can reach
the reality of the divine that she sees in Naomi's life, even
when Naomi complains about God's abandoning her.

With Ruth, "virginal" means something different from what
is usually associated with the fertility cults. It is something
closer to the welcoming chastity of Mary, the mother of Jesus.
Ruth, like Tamar and Rahab, is not a numinous figure in herself, not a goddess, not caught up in any way with cultic practice. All these ancestresses are mortal women, avatars of the
human at its extraordinary best.[24] Each plays a pivotal role in

creating and preserving the new humanity called Israel and the new being that Jesus will bring into it. They are links between the Chosen One and the world, foreign, as they must be, placed where they are, on borders between countries, between unfaith and faith, between barrenness and birth, between nothingness and the coming into being of the religion of the saving of races.

We see anticipated here Jesus' crossing of the borders that separate Jew and Gentile. Ruth's story is a prefiguration of Jesus' meeting with the Samaritan woman, of his calling of a hated tax collector to become his follower, of his love for the outcasts of society—whore, wanton, the unseemly poor, the unjust steward, the laborer who sneaks in at the last moment to demand his full wage. Ruth is linked to the Jesus who puzzles his disciples in his lavish defense of a mysterious woman who has poured costly ointment on his head to anoint him in preparation for his approaching death. "But she should have sold it and given the money to the poor!" the disciples protest. No. Out of the same kind of spiritually and psychologically virginal love that is in Ruth, thrusting aside the claims of the law, Jesus insists that she shall be called blessed.

No wonder the words of Ruth—"Entreat me not to leave thee, for whither thou goest I will go . . ."—are taken by couples as part of their marriage vows. For this level of love shows us something different from what we usually understand of a love between a daughter and a mother-in-law or a love that is anything like it. It defies logic and common sense. It is not concerned with approved boundaries of order that mark off the limits of the self, but rather with a lavish giving of self, an active surrender, a determined openness to being—and the fullness of being that comes with it—whether in the person of the God of Israel who so impresses Ruth or as the annunciating angel who addresses Mary. This is not a stranger coming to a temple votary whom she accepts as a god incarnate. This God who covenants with Israel has a name, the name of Being. So has the coming God, the fruit of Mary's womb. Tamar, Rahab, Ruth, Mary, each in her own way, struggles toward letting something happen in relation to this deeply planted God who speaks from within the flesh of an embodied experience—in conception, in pregnancy, in birth, in love, in valiant acts, yes, and in acts of adultery, treason, incest—showing the wisdom of the serpent and the cunning of the dove.

Ruth does what she does for love of another woman. This is the animating strength of Ruth as redeemer. It is what makes her a Christ figure. Ruth's devotion reaches below the conventions of collective consciousness to the hidden feminine values of love and faith that spring from unfamiliar depths in the collective unconscious where the spirit makes its presence felt and Being is defined. No man, not even Boaz, really shapes or extends this circle around Naomi and Ruth. (Some commentators say Boaz died the day after the wedding.[25]) The quality of their bonding transcends hierarchy and rules, country and custom, generations and faiths. It engenders courage. In it is a founding truth appropriate to its place in the history of Jesus.

This love of Ruth and Naomi goes beyond the distinction between subject and object that logical thinking insists on. Self knows itself in the other, as soul and world know themselves in each other. This is a knowing like that of contemplation. It is knowing as being.

Some relationships between women fall on the rocks because the two women lose hold of the transcendent element to which Ruth remained centrally committed. Then the circle of connection between the women becomes smaller and smaller as each forces upon the other projections that must ultimately be betrayed by the limits of finite being. Words of recrimination, broken trust, bruised feelings complete the downward spiral that narrows communication between them. Accusations that one has betrayed the other, or failed to heal her wounds, or renounced her pledge of constancy, or dishonored her most tender needs are tossed back and forth. The deep love of one woman for another that Ruth shows here becomes a fruitless merger where each participant seeks to become lost in the other. Then, inexorably, they must split from each other, be torn apart to find again the self each is given to be and to give, which cannot be demanded, even in such a closeness of relationship.

Relationships between human beings must always fall on the rocks when they lose sight of the transcendent element that their love first opened them to perceive and to serve. The love degenerates into hostile polarization, characterized by an exaggerated sense of function and distance, and ends in absolute incomprehension of what makes a person—oneself, the other—tick.[26]

The issue between Ruth and Naomi is not sexual. It is what undergirds the sexual and what springs from the feminine, whether it is lived in relationships between women, between women and men, or between men. It is the quality that defines Ruth's role as redeemer.

Despite the depth of Ruth's feeling and determination, a shadowy side of sexuality hovers over this story. Here, Ruth is like Tamar, though in the latter's narrative the theme appears more boldly. It is incest I am talking about. Tamar consciously and purposefully engages her father-in-law in a sexual meeting. Ruth's relation with Boaz is perhaps not technically incest, for the kinship between them is too far removed. But Boaz calls Ruth "daughter" (2:8, 3:10, 11), and the elders recommend that his house be seen, in effect, like that of Tamar and Judah (4:12). Boaz, in fact, is descended from the incestuous coupling of Judah and Tamar, and Ruth from the incestuous congress of Lot and his daughter. At the end of all this incestuous inbreeding, from Ruth and Boaz, will be born Obed, the grandfather of King David and ancestor of the Messiah. What are we to make of this theme of incest in the genealogical line of Jesus?

Looked at reductively, incest is a crime, one long held to be so in human history. In ancient times, it was taboo; for centuries it was considered a cause of retardation and insanity. In our own century Freud investigated its interdiction as the root of the Oedipal conflict that every one of us must pass through. Failure to do so results in psychosis.[27] We remain within the parent-child orbit; we are unable to acquire our own range of being (complete with the distinctions and differentiations on which language and thought are based), which will enable us to become separate subjects. Instead we persist in feeling ourselves the object of others' thoughts and feelings and see them merely as characters in our own fantasies. More recent work on incest underscores its most severe effects: its victim may suffer dissociation to the point of splitting into multiple personalities.[28] Such a person's memory, burdened by intolerably painful incidents of sexual invasion, proves faulty, spotty, inadequate in its self-censoring. One seems mad to oneself and to others; therefore, little coherence can be brought even to recounting what happened. A terrible fear persists: Did I make it all up? Am I exaggerating? And then there is the accompanying shame: Was it my fault? Did I contribute to it? Altogether, the victim falls into abysmal confusion. Consciousness cannot contain the trauma, so a beleaguered unconscious holds it instead; the trauma manifests in bodily symptoms, sexual dysfunction, and a dreadful sense that one's personality is not whole, but broken up into warring fragments. How, then, can this incest theme be part of the Christ's heritage? Is it something that Jesus must redeem and heal?

Looked at symbolically, incest gathers another significance. The *Zohar*, the mystical Kabbalist book, sees the incest of Tamar and Judah as ordained by God. This calls to mind the mythic motif of the *hieros gamos*, the union of opposites from which a divine child will be born.[29] One of the principal divisions between Freud and Jung was Jung's adding to the meaning of the Oedipal conflict this symbolic reading of incest. While not rejecting Freud's emphasis upon the regressive interpretation of Oedipal wishes—to become the sexual partner and total center of attention of our parent—Jung adds a further symbolic interpretation.[30] Here the longing for parent is a longing for what a parent symbolizes: first, the security, innocence, protection, and love of childhood; second, our longing for wholeness. These psychic longings for security and wholeness insistently grab our attention through their sexual charge.[31] The other that we long for symbolizes a contrasexual part of ourselves, that is, an unconscious part of us quite opposite to our conscious gender identity.[32] In coming together with this other, we begin to feel united within. This is "union with one's own being," finding how to put together into a whole all the parts of ourselves that the sexual symbolizes so well.[33] As Jung puts it, the longing for "union on the biological level is a symbol of the *unio oppositorum* at its highest."[34] It also underlines the fact that we cannot become whole, complete in ourselves, without being involved with other persons.

Can we then surmise that, on the human level, the incest theme in both the Tamar and Ruth narratives draws upon this symbolic meaning of the urge to make whole? And on the divine level, the incest prefigures the uniting of opposing masculine and feminine elements of being that will produce a Savior in whom both elements are not only included but fulfilled?

Before Boaz can claim Ruth as his bride, another kinsman

must be faced. Here Boaz becomes a trickster in order to force
Naomi's nearest kinsman by marriage to renounce his prior
right to buy the land Naomi inherited from her husband Elimelech's family. Being in no position to work the land, Naomi
has not benefited from it. But in this agricultural community,
her kinsman sees its value. He wants to purchase the land but
does not want to marry Ruth or to pay the expense of developing the land for Ruth and her mother-in-law, unless in the
end it will pay him and his own direct heirs. When he hears
that the land will revert to Ruth's and hence to Elimelech's
heirs, he quits the claim. Boaz thus can use the intricacies of
the law to make Ruth his wife without alienating either her or
himself from the surrounding clan society.[35] He does his ne-
gotiation openly, before witnesses at the city gate. Who is this
kinsman Boaz confronts? We know nothing of him, not even
his name, but we do understand his attitude. It is straightfor-
wardly materialistic. He will take the land of Elimelech—following an old orientation that was exclusively of the Hebrew
faith—but he will not follow the new orientation that will include Ruth, the alien feminine, and then raise with her "a new
heir for the old heritage."[36]

We can surmise that this "nearest kinsman" might represent
a shadow part of Boaz that balks at accepting and reintegrating
a "previously repressed feminine element."[37] The shadow is
that part of each of us that we keep hidden in the unconscious,
not wanting or fearing to own it.[38] Before Boaz can bring this
new feminine element into the center of Hebrew faith publicly—that is, under the law, consciously and clearly within
the community as represented by the public gate—he must
confront and deal with a less savory part of himself. This part
belongs to Boaz as wealthy landowner, one who, like his kinsman, can see a good deal in acquiring more property. But that
motive for marrying Ruth must be put aside. Boaz differenti-

ates his feelings from the materialistic bias. He chooses Ruth freely and decisively, drawing off his shoe to confirm the contract—that is, taking off and putting on again a symbol of his standpoint (and, in those times, a sign of liberty and freedom, as slaves went barefoot) to indicate that he is binding himself to this new agreement.[39] Boaz chooses Ruth out of gratitude and a real sense of her redemptive power.

Ruth foreshadows Christ the redeemer in her identifying with the relict at the bottom of the heap, the remnant of the remnant.[40] She allies herself with a single old woman who, in a patriarchal society, is without power or position. This is what Jesus experienced—born in the muck of a stable, living his life with nowhere to lay his head, a constant example that God moves through the left-out and forsaken parts of us to bring wholeness to all.

Twice in this remarkable tale Ruth is shown as a channel of grace. When she comes to work for him, Boaz hails her, like the angel of the annunciation speaking to Mary, as one worthy of the fullest reward from "the Lord God of Israel, under whose wings thou art come to trust" (2:12). When he wakes up to find her lying at his feet she responds by identifying herself and inviting him to spread his skirt—his wings—over his "handmaid," in the clearest adumbration of Mary's magnificat. Boaz thanks her and blesses her for her *chesed*, her loving-kindness (3:9–10). Ruth's kindness, her *chesed*, echoes the word used again and again in the Hebrew Bible to describe Yahweh's own loving bestowal. Her redemptive offering is protected by the Lord God of Israel in the shelter of his wings, and Boaz's skirt—the word is the same in the Hebrew text—under which she seeks haven.[41] Ruth prefigures Christ as mother bird: "How often would I have gathered your children together as a hen gathers her brood under her wings" (Matt. 23:37). Like Jesus, Ruth moves from emptiness to fullness, from death to life, from no future to total faith and hope, from bitterness to gratitude. God hides, we are reminded, in the remnant, in the weak, performing the drama of salvation through the persons and events least likely to become channels of grace.[42]

In the *Zohar* version of Ruth, she is seen as personifying both the community of Israel and the Shekinah, the feminine side of God in Kabbalist doctrines. So in her coming together with Boaz, whose name means "in him is strength" and who represents God as the Redeemer of Israel, we see represented the redeeming strengths of the feminine.[43] Even more, we may add, in recovering this lost mite, the feminine manifests God's wholeness.

In this story Ruth begins her redeeming action forthrightly, and others quickly catch on. Like her sisters Tamar and Rahab, she assumes the role of intercessor, and its contagious quality is revealed dramatically in what follows. Ruth redeems Naomi by insisting on accompanying her, by providing her food, and finally giving her a home and a child. Boaz deepens the redemptive drama by taking Ruth under his protection and then, for Ruth as his wife, recovering her land and her name for her. Ruth chooses his shelter and protection, electing him as sexual partner, giving him a son, evoking in him a steadfast kindness, a God-like *chesed*. She redeems all of us, in truth, for from her come kings and prophets and "all the boons and all the consolations which the Holy One, blessed be he, is destined to bestow on Solomon."[44] In Ruth, we learn the great truth that we are, each of us, agents of each other's salvation, spiritually and psychologically.

FIVE

BATHSHEBA

BATHSHEBA'S STORY IS TOLD in several texts: 2 Samuel 11–12; 1 Kings 1:11–21, 28–31; 2:13–21; and 1 Chronicles 3:5. While walking in the late afternoon on the roof of his house, King David spies "a woman bathing . . . the women was very beautiful" (2 Sam. 11:2). He asks who she is and learns that she is Bathsheba, daughter of Eliam (meaning "God is gracious") and wife of Uriah the Hittite. Seeing her beauty, David fills with desire. He sends for her and quickly takes her: "She came to him, and he lay with her" (2 Sam. 11:4). The text notes that at the time "she was purifying herself from her uncleanness" (2 Sam. 11:4). Then Bathsheba returns to her home. Sometime later, she discovers that she has conceived and sends word to David: "I am with child" (2 Sam. 11:5).

Uriah is fighting in David's army,which is besieging Rabbah, the Ammonite capital. David summons Uriah home on the pretext of trying to learn how the war is going. He urges Uriah to return to see his wife and spend the night with her, even sending a present with him. But Uriah insists on sleeping at the door of the king's house, with all his other servants. David protests. Uriah declares that while the Ark and Israel and Judah dwell in booths, and the army camps in open fields, he will not go home, eat, drink, and lie with his wife. David asks him then to remain and eat and drink with him. David succeeds in making Uriah drunk, but still Uriah will not go down to his wife; again, he sleeps with David's servants.

David then sends Uriah back to battle with a sealed note to his commander, Joab, instructing him to put Uriah at the front, in the fiercest fighting. Uriah, as a result, is slain. Joab sends David a messenger, instructing him that if David grows angry when he hears of the valiant men lost in battle and protests that Joab should not have let the men go so near the city wall, the messenger should tell the king that Uriah the Hittite is also dead.

The "wife of Uriah," as she is named at this point in the text, hearing that her husband is dead, laments for him. When her mourning is done, David makes her his wife and she bears him a son.

But the Lord, we learn, is displeased with David and sends the wise man Nathan to remonstrate with him. Asking David to fulfill the role of a high-court judge, Nathan sets before him the following case. A rich man has many flocks and herds but nevertheless steals the one little ewe lamb that belongs to a poor man who has raised the lamb and fed it and thinks of it as a daughter. What should be done after such an act? David answers angrily that the man should die. Nathan then speaks famous words: "Thou are the man!" (2 Sam. 12:7). For look, here is David, whom Yahweh delivered from the hand of Saul and made king over Israel, to whom he gave many wives, and yet he must take the one and only wife of Uriah, a loyal servant, and see that he is slain with the sword of the Ammonites. Nathan pronounces Yahweh's judgment: The sword will never depart from your kingdom. Another will take your wives before your eyes and lie with them in the light of the sun. You will not die, but because you scorned the Lord, your son will.

The prophecy comes true. The little son of David and Bathsheba falls sick and dies. David's kingdom is divided. His sons

war against each other, and finally Absalom sleeps with David's wives in full daylight on the roof of David's house and tries
to steal the kingdom from his father. David cannot act decisively, because his moral sense is so greatly weakened by his
own sin. He cannot punish others without himself seeming
unjust and hypocritical; he himself has committed the injus-
tices he judges in others. He has lost all ability to understand
the dual responsibility that rests with him as father and king.
He spends the next twenty-two years repenting daily for his
rebellion against God. Finally, when David is old and dying,
Nathan sends Bathsheba—now called by her name in the
text—to tell the king that still another son, Adonijah, seeks to
steal his kingdom. Will he not put their second son, Solomon,
on the throne? David agrees; Bathsheba bows in reverence. Solomon reigns and places Bathsheba on his right as honored
queen mother.

Bathsheba has a special place indeed among the ancestresses
of Jesus. For we see her only through the eyes of others. Like
her sisters, she is a foreigner, because of her marriage to a
Hittite, but she is also foreign in a different sense. We do not
hear her voice. She is all but mute. We hear her speak only
twice, when she sends word to David that she is pregnant and
when she asks David to make Solomon his successor as king of
Israel. In Bathsheba, we see how a man experiences a woman
as foreign to himself and what happens to him as a result.
Bathsheba brings into the line of Jesus the element of woman
in man, woman seen by man, woman who changes man,
woman disposed of by man. Only at the end of this tale does
Bathsheba act—and even then, on the advice of a man, Nathan, and for the sake of a man, Solomon. We do not see her
as the maker of this story but only through the eyes of the man
David and what his experience of her makes of him.

Bathsheba herself remains foreign to us, the readers of the biblical text. Though she acts as the center of David's story, as the precipitating cause of his temptation, his fall, his repentance, and his redemption—we never hear her story directly. In this way, Bathsheba is also foreign to the other female ancestors. For each of them was the clear subject of her own story. Bathsheba is never subject, only the object of a man whose fate she determines and whose fate seals her own. Whom she desires, what she thinks or plots or repents, we never know.

Bathsheba might be taken to represent all those voiceless women who are perceived only as objects of men's responses. Granted that Bathsheba is perceived by David as most beautiful and desirable, hence a positive object—still, object she remains. She is not so distant from those many other women who are perceived by men as ugly, bad, even dreadful—in a word, as negative objects.

Bathsheba can be taken to symbolize woman as the forgotten subject. This symbolization instructs us in the frightful consequences of denying woman her rightful place in her own story. Not only is she moved around like a pawn, a mere adjunct to the king's subjectivity, but the king's appropriating of her is judged by God as sin, as flaw, as the weak place, the rent in the whole fabric of the ruling orientation of consciousness and, through David, what David represents as king of all of Israel. The feminine is not seen in its own right, embodied here by the woman Bathsheba, but seen only as satellite to a masculine consciousness. Hence it cannot exert its influence directly and freely, but can only serve as a channel for events in and through a man.

The results for the kingdom—the lives of countless others as well as the kingdom's ruling attitude—are disastrous. The kingdom is split in two. David's son Absalom vies with his father for power. Instead of renewing his aging father with a new spirit linked to the old, the son seeks to defeat and kill the father, and the father seeks to kill his son, albeit reluctantly, for David loves Absalom. Symbolically, then, we may say that when the feminine element does not receive its due recognition and enter into the story as a free and equal subject, but instead is treated only as adjunct to male, as object, then there must result an either/or disruption of a whole state—whether of consciousness or of kingdom. We might surmise that had the feminine been included as subject, renewal of the kingdom and of the ruling consciousness might have proceeded along both/and lines. This interpretation of the superseding of violence over regeneration is underlined by the subplot of Absalom's uprising against David for control of the kingdom. Absalom's brother Ammon has raped their sister Tamar, over her great protests that if he applied to King David, their father, she could be given to him. After his crime, Ammon compounds insult and injury by utterly repudiating Tamar. Absalom engineers Ammon's death in revenge for his violence against Tamar. David is unable to act or react decisively, he is so hobbled by his own unjust actions. And so the son begins his revolt in the name of avenging the feminine, and the father must let the uprising accumulate strength because of his own crimes, precipitated by the feminine. It is no small thing to neglect feminine elements. The story tells us that everybody pays when that occurs.

When we first see Bathsheba, we are immediately aware of the power of the human eye, both literally and symbolically, both looking within and looking at another; we see the seeing that is filled with eros.[1] This is how Bathsheba enters the story. We see David's seeing her.

In the psychological investigation of dream symbols, the eye often stands for the sexual organs, as here, where the immediate result of David's seeing Bathsheba is his lying with her. Eros has an emotional quality that quickly becomes a staring at and contemplation of an object. Erotic emotion produces a heightened consciousness of an object and illuminates the seer, as David is illuminated by Bathsheba. She fills him as he gazes at her. She penetrates him before he enters her. His gazing at her puts him under her spell so that he loses consciousness of everything else. Fixing his stare upon her, David fills with his libido, makes her pregnant with it.[2] Thus compelled, he must send for her and take her.

The text hints at another dread power Bathsheba possesses. She is purifying herself from her "uncleanness," which is to say her menstrual period. The taboo around woman's blood-food stands behind the Jewish ritual of *mikvah*, the ritual bath, and also stands behind the churching of women after child-birth. In this taboo a woman's blood represents a demonic nonhuman aspect of the female, connected to cold-blooded instinct. It symbolizes both mana and evil; it is both life-giving, and thus to be respected, and polluting, thus to be avoided. In ancient times it was feared that the effect of a bleeding woman on a man was to arouse untamed desire, like an animal in heat calling all males to her backyard. A man might then forget all his other duties, lose his precarious ego-consciousness, or be made impotent. The allusion to Bathsheba's period suggests this dread aspect of the female, just as with Tamar the death-dealing effects of intercourse are pointed to.[3] This suggestion of the dread of menstrual blood in Bathsheba is met directly with Jesus' healing powers, which extend even to mental attitudes. He is not afraid of woman's blood, but moves to heal the woman touching him in a crowd, who has been hemor-rhaging for twelve years. And he does not begrudge the woman her healing even though she has stolen it from him (Matt. 9:20–22).

Bathsheba's beauty has such power for David that he forgets all his duties, obligations, passions, faithfulness as king. In clinical practice I have more than once come across a man for whom a woman's beauty has carried the power of the transcendent. The man falls numb, mute, is unable to speak, sometimes even to move. He feels bewitched.[4] The sheer beauty of the woman—her smile, the luminosity of her skin, the blue of her eyes, or, like the goddess Artemis for Actaeon as he spies on her, the beauty of her body as she bathes—transfixes his senses and paralyzes his capacity to reason and communicate. He looks; he stares. He stands or kneels in awe. Her beauty manifests the ineffable presence of divinity. In Bathsheba's story we see again the capacity of beauty to mediate to us the religious dimension of the arts, and the religious dimension of voyeurism. God comes to us in many different ways. Beauty, for some of us, is a principal revelation of the divine. See this passage from Elizabeth Längasser's novel, *The Quest:*

> She is gazing at a milk-white stone whose color is of great simplicity and whose surface is of an enchanting smoothness. This color forces its way into the being of the child with the violence of a revelation, a pure, direct vision of absolute beauty. . . . She becomes absorbed in its quiet radiance, and slips into that long-forgotten, magical rhythm that brings her into harmony with existence, and which, though she cannot know it, is the rhythm of the spheres. . . . She enters effortlessly into the pleasure of perfect freedom.[5]

Consider the depiction of the female body in Western culture as it has been used for centuries, as a means of concretizing, of making palpable the presence of the transcendent in the finite.[6]

As for pathology, sometimes the numinous chooses it to

make itself known. The voyeur suffers an invasion of the other through the eye at the same time as he invades the other with his eye. This affliction bespeaks religious, not sexual, repression. For in addition to invasion of the person that voyeurism represents, where a man doubts his capacity to feel present and potent before a beautiful woman, the voyeur is caught in a displacement of worship.[7] Truth, beauty, and goodness are eternal verities, interwoven with each other. For some, God is manifest especially through beauty. Their soul is captured, but they do not recognize what has happened, do not see through the beauty its source in God. Repressed religious desire is translated into sexual terms only. The rituals of voyeurism, which often include complicated devices for viewing and masturbation, comprise a compulsive substitute for rituals of meditation on the transcendent and ways the soul can pour itself out in adoration.

When the voyeuristic problem is resolved, a man may still find beauty his connection to the divine. To recover to consciousness his religious longings is not to dispense with the awe inspired in him by a woman's beauty. Rather, it puts the awe in a wider perspective that gives space to a man's sexual appreciation of a beautiful woman and a dwelling in his soul for appreciation of what she symbolizes. Now he can consciously worship the divine through a woman's beauty, instead of falling captive to the beauty, often, as David's story shows, with disastrous results for her as well as for him.

We see in David's enraptured gazing, and in the religious aspect of his voyeuristic maneuvering, the instinctive basis of religious ritual, the precious core of religious practice. Religion that is alive and real is not some ethereal, world-denying escape from physicality, but rather is body-based, all the way down into our instinctual life. Rooted there, religion includes guts, teeth, orgasms, all fixed in the profound motions of the soul. There grew up spontaneously in the Middle Ages the practice of elevating the Eucharist after the consecration, so that it might be seen by all. This "Voir Dieu" rite dramatized the climax of worship. People took in the host by seeing it; they incorporated divinity through their eyes.[8]

Most times when a man is so caught by a woman whom he eyes, he does not know that she bears the transcendent toward him. All he knows is that he must have her. He projects his own soul onto her and then cannot live without her, just as he cannot live without his soul. She is the link to all that matters. Entering her, he enters the heart of darkness at the center of being. Touching her, he touches the pulse at the center. Who she is in herself does not matter. And so the text never asks what Bathsheba feels for David or in response to his peremptory summons, or about her husband's killing or her baby's death. A man sees the woman as his eye beholds her. Onto her, he fixes his own unconscious emotions, his intimations of the eternal. She carries his projected soul, though she remains unknown in herself, almost a collective figure. He identifies her with his projections and does not inquire into her subjectivity.[9]

Because David is king and symbolizes the conscious orientation that reigns over his whole society, his projective identification of his soul with Bathsheba suggests that she represents the unintegrated soul-aspect of the kingdom, which is here linked to the voiceless foreign feminine.

We do not know anything of Bathsheba's experiences or feelings because we read only of David's responses. A woman can only too easily be tempted to allow herself to be defined by a man's projections and his imposition of an identity. A woman who accepts a man's projections as her self-definition finds herself identified with his female element, with his anima, in Jung's vocabulary. This may happen to her involuntarily because she is unconscious of herself, or she may intentionally set out to capture the man's projections in order to gain power over him. She comes alive, then, only in terms of his image of her, of his own feminine nature, however little differentiated or accepted. A woman who attracts such projections finds herself, sooner or later, facing an ethical question about how to carry or reject or return such parts of a man without exploiting him. [10]

A particular problem—a wonderful possibility, really— arises for a beautiful woman or a woman for whom beauty manifests the transcendent. She can learn how to relate to this endowment, carry it, tend to it, be glad in it and suffer the weight of it, return it to its source, by knowing all the time, and insisting on remembering, that beauty comes from God, that she did not create it by herself. Then she must also stand up for it. Once, as an analysand talked about her worries about her little daughter's behavior and guiding values, she mentioned with some feeling her child's great love of pretty clothes, her demand for them. It was a love of beauty that her mother shared. I said, in effect, "And you are finding your way to communicate that clothes are not the important value?" After a pause, the woman said quietly, "But they are." And I saw that I had not adequately received what fine fabrics, graceful lines, and sensuous textures communicated to her—the impact of beauty that mediated the essence of life to her.

When women push away the identities imposed on them by men and seek to discover for themselves who they are underneath it all, there is a great advance in consciousness and a convulsive change in the surrounding culture. For when a woman returns to a man his projected feminine part of himself, he must deal with it. The image he projects may be of the traditional wife-mother-helpmate. It may be the sexual siren, who is thought evil in her designs to ensnare men, or the idealized spiritual madonna. It may be mystery incarnate, the unselfconscious instinctual life of a femininity that never knows beforehand what it is or wants but just waits, silent and ambiguous, until a man forces his imprint upon it. Whatever a man's image of woman, in large part it is his alone; it belongs to him and he must face and integrate it as part of his own personality. He must stop asking women to be its carrier. Women, freed to be themselves, can then return to men the energy that is men's alone to deal with.

Women can then take up the task of inquiring into and shaping their own choices and options. Too often their temptation is to dodge the task in loud protest against imposed roles or forced submission, rather than to originate or select desirable opportunities. This rearrangement of energy is the psychological issue that hides in the cultural pressures on men to help with housework and child-rearing. The disidentification of woman and the feminine from maternal instinct is the great magnetic psychological force that lies behind the abortion issue.

Hidden in such changes in personal and cultural consciousness, where a woman no longer allows herself to be defined by men's projections and where a man must face the female element in himself, is a religious issue. Bathsheba's story focuses on this issue, which a man must himself face, as prompted by the feminine in himself. A man can be gripped by a woman, just as David was compelled toward Bathsheba. Then through his eye the deepest intent of his heart has awakened. He desires; he intends; he reaches toward. He is pulled out of himself. Gregory the Great compares the interior of the eye to the heavenly home of the Holy Spirit.[11] The lover of the Song of Songs speaks of his beloved's dove eyes, thus combining in one image the bird of Aphrodite and the symbol of the Holy Spirit. In terms of modern depth psychology, this amounts to saying that through the feminine aspect of the man's psyche, his anima, is mediated the light of the Self, that center of all the personality, conscious and unconscious, that transcends the ego and that gives it a first experience of transcendence. [12]

The Self is not God in us, but rather that in us that knows about God. In the Bathsheba text we learn that man is awakened to the Self through the sharp, bidding beauty of the feminine part of himself. It—she—brings him to the experience of a state in which the "I" and the "other" are brought together, are both the same and not the same at once. This is a small but powerful version, a beginning one, of the mystical state that Saint Paul describes as "I and yet not I but Christ who lives in me."

If we ignore the sexual root of the highest contemplative union with God, our religion will become diluted, grow bloodless, without passion or permanence. We cannot make up in ethical maxim or political exhortation what we have lost in primary soul experience. That reverses the two great commandments, putting love of neighbor and of self ahead of the all-out lavish loving of God with everything of our heart, mind, body, and strength.

In the story of Bathsheba, we learn both where a man goes off and falls away from this spiritual opportunity, and why, at the deepest level of their lives, what women are after is spiritual development. Instead of letting the anima image illuminate his consciousness with the light of the Self, a man defective in this way equates woman with the source of light and thereby falls into idolatry. She becomes a stand-in for God, to her peril, to his, and to ours. As the source of forbidden desires that have entered through his eye, she is to be blamed as the evil one, as history again and again sadly witnesses, in witch burnings, wife beatings, and the sin and crime of rape, which is both sexual and violent, for it is an intentional attack on a woman's sexual center—her eye, the eye of her vulva.[13] Or equally sadly, a woman remains the source of all good, forced by a man onto a pedestal, an inhuman idol. A man caught up in such idolatry fails to see that in his woman and through her it is God calling to him and touching his innermost heart.

What lies behind the stalemate situation of a man caught between two women, often enough a wife and a mistress, where he can neither leave nor fully join either one, is an issue of soul. The man's soul, like the womanly element inside him, may be trying to reach him, first through one woman, then through the other. His way out of such a stalemate, which must end by hurting at least three people, and more, if there are children and grandparents in the mix, is to look for the inner woman trying to show him something about the larger Self that lies within his reach. She is the way to God, just as Sophia was for Jacob Boehme.[14]

When a man and a woman notice that projections are flying back and forth between them, then a big middle space opens. In that space, many conversations may occur—between the two people; between the woman and what she projects onto the man, with him listening in; between the man and what he projects onto the woman, with her listening in; between the projected contents, the two soul-complexes; and between all of the above and the Self-center, that is, that which bids them to their own depths and to what transcends them. This series of conversations resounds with the hum of being.[15] But, too often, we split up the parts and stop up the flow of conversation. We turn away.

In biblical terms, sin, that turning away, is to take the means for the end, to see the woman instead of God. Yahweh says it plainly to David: Because you despised me and took Uriah's wife, I will raise up evil against you. And David answers plainly: I have sinned against the Lord. The issue lies first between Yahweh and David. Yahweh says, in effect: Why didn't you choose me? Why her instead of me? Why didn't you see through her to me? Yahweh loves with a lover's passion for his beloved. And David sees that this is so and acknowledges his guilt.

The text leads us to the mystery of sin. Why can't we see God's hand reaching out to us in what tempts us? Seeing this, David might still have sent for Bathsheba, but he would have done so with a very different consciousness. There lies the difference. Jesus said: The one who is close to me is close to the fire, and if you know what you do, you are blessed; but if you know not, then you are cursed.[16] For David to see Yahweh through Bathsheba's mediating presence would have meant to suffer those opposing pulls consciously. His task would have been to probe the exchanges to see what action should follow, to renounce Bathsheba or to take her. But David just substituted Bathsheba's lures for the compelling power of God, and identified her with what looked into him through her, thereby causing endless unconscious suffering, what we traditionally have called innocent suffering. What led up to this?

What woke David up to this trouble was Bathsheba's simple words: I am with child. The fear of pregnancy, the consequence of pregnancy, has had so much to answer for through the ages! David tries to weasel his way out by tricking Uriah into intercourse with his wife. Then the child could be passed off as his. But another stronger element enters, Uriah's righteousness.

Here what is good, moving, and full of honor contributes to what is bad. David's guile is caught out by its opposite in Uriah, an unbending honor. Uriah cannot think of pleasuring himself when the Ark of Yahweh goes into battle. He cannot gratify himself when other soldiers are fighting the king's war. Behind his noble words of refusal lurks another fear perhaps.

Intercourse with a woman might steal his soldier's valor, his courage, his power to fight.[17] Though Bathsheba's voice is mute, her presence here, behind the scenes, thunders with power. The same fear of entering woman that we found in the Tamar story turns up again now with Bathsheba.

Is Uriah too unbending, too fixed in his purity? We hear nothing of temptation or wish, nothing of ambivalence or complexity. Is Uriah telling us of the perils of idealizing our goal and of our commitment to it—that such idealizing single-mindedness can seal our death warrant? David uses Uriah himself to carry his death warrant in the note he sends with him to Joab. Uriah never suspects the king, never raises any questions about David's persistent urging him to see his wife. He apparently sees nothing wrong in David calling him back from the front. Perhaps because Uriah found no mixed motives in himself, he could find none in another. If we do not see into the underside of our own badness, what Jung calls our shadow, that which lies outside the clear light of our ego but still follows us around, we cannot see the shadows of others, let alone protect ourselves against them.[18]

David was all shadow in his interchange with Uriah, Uriah without any shadow in his dealings with David. David tried to gain Bathsheba by denying his shadow, symbolized by Uriah. Uriah tried to keep Bathsheba by denying his shadow, that is, David. In one, the shadow holds all the denied, upright, honorable goodness; in the other it holds all the tricky angling and the manipulation for one's own ends alone. David's tricks fail, unlike the tricks of the female ancestors, all of which prevail. Why? Was it because each woman knew what wrong she had committed and for what right end? David knew only wrong, Uriah only right. The link of the mediating feminine between them was missing, for Bathsheba had no voice and was never seen as herself.

The result of David's sin is that the innocent must suffer. This may be an answer to Job's question about the root of undeserved suffering and to all of us who ask why children, sleeping innocently in their beds, die from drug dealers' gunshots flying through the walls and windows of their apartments, or why children are born into countries where the earth has been parched for decades and the government refuses for political reasons to distribute food to all its citizens.

Why do the innocent suffer? Because that is how sin works. The inextricable web of interdependence holds all of us, old and young, near neighbor and far, innocent and guilty, male and female, when any one of us falls. The shock effect is felt by the last little one. David's and Bathsheba's child dies. Uriah dies. The kingdom falls apart. Many, many must die.

The worst fact of sin is what it does, not just to those of us who commit the sins, but to those who have nothing to do with our sins. Like the deep red stain of wine spilled on a white cloth, sin's stains cannot be confined to just one patch of fabric, just one thin layer; they spread; they seep; they color every part of our lives.[19] Sin affects all of our lives, reaches across peoples and nations, across worlds, across eras, across past and future. We act out our mother's neglect of us in roiling complexes of envy and hate that we put into the world. We cannot help but deprive our children, our friends, our neighbors, as we have been deprived. This is reason enough for intercessory prayer—not only for the living neighbor, but for the dead one and all who will come after.

Jesus' blood and the memorial wine of the Eucharist staunch stains of sin—blood for blood. They, the blood and the wine that becomes the blood, pull us into the currents of God's love as it flows into the world. Only voluntary suffering on behalf of sinners can save us from the permanent stains of sin.

David's sin costs Israel everything. Bathsheba's story tells us that and much else. Because of Bathsheba, a king changes and the conception of a king changes. That change is fulfilled in the king that her son Solomon came to be. David himself changes from warrior king, from self-righteous king, to penitent king, changes from Israel's almighty monarch to a wounded one, a king of power to a religious one. David is thought to be the author of the great penitential Psalm 51: "Wash me thoroughly from mine iniquity, and cleanse me from my sin. For I acknowledge my transgressions: my sin is ever before me" (51:2–3). In some legends, God himself is thought to bring David to his crime so that because of him the Deity may say to other sinners, "Go to David and learn how to repent."[20]

If we understand the king psychologically as representing the ruling consciousness of a kingdom and a people, we can understand the change in David as a growth in Israel's consciousness. The ego of the kingdom changes, moves closer to the Self. At first, there is an ego that forgets its origins in Self and its role to serve the psyche as a whole. Then, after Bathsheba, we find a king who repents daily before God, who daily seeks renewal in Self. David manifests God's call not for a human sacrifice, but for a contrite spirit.

In *The Legends of the Jews* the story is told that David showed enormous pride and self-righteousness when he complained to Yahweh that no one said "the God of David" the way they had said "the God of Abraham, God of Jacob, God of Isaac." God responds: But you have not been proven as they were. David says: Try me. God responds: Yes, and I shall even grant you what I did not grant the patriarchs—I will tell you beforehand that you will fall into temptation through a woman. Satan appears to David in the form of a bird. To protect himself, David throws a dart at Satan. But it misses and instead breaks a piece from a wicker screen behind which he sees Bathsheba.[21] What a drama! What directness and clarity of response!

What do we learn from the drama? That sin comes. That we need to pay attention and not think we can outwit it in toe-to-toe struggle. The very defense David makes against Satan by throwing his dart at the bird turns out to be precisely what leads him to Bathsheba. David's subsequent conduct hints at a further answer. We cannot protect ourselves by or in ourselves. We must look daily to God, pray daily to God, and repent as often before God. We come into the world with nothing. Everything we have is given us, even the power to work for what we have; we must daily remember to give it all back, give it all up in a lavish outpouring of loving God, with our whole heart and mind and soul and strength. Only then, loving God with all of ourself, can we love our neighbor as we love ourself.

At the end of the story, Bathsheba speaks. She asks that Solomon be made king after David. And so it is done. And Solomon becomes the one who knows what David learned from his sin with Bathsheba. For when God asks what Solomon wants God to give him, Solomon answers: An understanding heart and wise counsel. Here is a son who has taken up with wisdom and understanding the legacy of his father's penitence. Solomon knows about shadowy motives, knows about the power and penetration of wisdom through a woman's beauty.

Because of Bathsheba, a major reorientation in consciousness occurs, from ego-king to Self-king, from king preoccupied with himself and his kingdom to king occupied with God first and last. She is where she belongs in the ancestry of Christ.

SIX

CONCLUSION

W HAT CONCLUSIONS ARE possible about these female ancestors of Christ? They come before David;
they come before Mary, the fifth of the mothers of
Christ, to whom there come as a result many intangible but
deeply felt legacies. But we should be specific about what
flows from these female ancestors into Jesus' tree of life.

It must be repeated: very little attention has been paid to
these four women as, in effect, Jesus' progenitors. In traditional theory, these women are included in the holy genealogy,
first, because they were sinners, and sexual sinners at that, and
thus their inclusion foreshadows Jesus' role as savior and provides a sort of apologetic to answer the claim made by some
Jews that Mary was an adulteress. Second, all these women
were aliens in Judea, and so, as Matthew emphasizes, Jesus,
the Jewish Messiah, was thus related in his ancestry to the
Gentiles. The third theory is closest to my own; it asserts that
all four, like Mary, knew irregular and scandalous union with
their partners, the first three showing unusual initiative in
working to reach their goals, and the fourth, Bathsheba, showing the radical effect of a woman on a man and, through him,
upon a whole society. These women are examples of the un-
expected means God uses to triumph over obstacles and to
prepare the way for the Messiah. Their scandalous behavior
both forecasts and supports Mary's scandalous pregnancy.[1]

For me, why these women appear in the genealogy of Jesus and why so little attention is paid to them is explained in the nature of what they bequeath to the Christ figure. Their legacy is relevant to human needs at any time and especially apposite for us in this last decade of a century and of a millennium. We know that these scandalous women are also self-confident; they are tricky, formidable, vital, single-minded, ingenious, always in some way related to the joining of sexuality and spirituality. Tamar is taken for a prostitute and commits incest; Rahab is a whore and a traitor; Ruth is a seducer; Bathsheba, an adulteress. All four, as with Mary in her illegitimate pregnancy, stand off-center in fixing the theme of the feminine at the center of messianic preparation. Each bears a new seed, opening to God's power in the conception of new being in the Christ. All of them make us look at Christianity in a different way. They introduce a counterorder into the mainstream, a different mind, a new way to apprehend what is revealed in God's coming. These women are border figures, new mixtures of old ingredients. That makes them fearful, close to the witch figure noted for stirring up trouble with her new potions, her insistent introduction into consciousness of what we usually prefer to repress.[2]

These women combine what Christian tradition usually separates — the fulfillment of the personal alongside the fulfillment of the holy. Too often in religious education we are instructed to deny the self and seek God, forgetting that it is God who gives us this self that wants to be alive and real and generous in its enjoyment of life. Irenaeus got it straight in his oft-quoted remark that the glory of God is human beings fully alive. But too often we inflict upon ourselves and upon those we love the idea that seeking self-satisfaction is selfish, sinful, oppressive of others, that only sacrifice of self really serves others. We forget the order of the Second Commandment and that we have nothing to give our neighbor if we do not love ourselves.

The four ancestresses bring into Jesus Christ's lineage the bold affirmation that we fulfill God's will when we pursue our vocation—God's direct will for each of us. Tamar, obsessed to conceive a child, redeems Judah's guilt for his treatment of Joseph and recovers the holy line to David from which Jesus sprang. Rahab, bent on self-preservation, not only saves her large number of kin but also exemplifies how faith and works combine, which is later to stand fully revealed in Christ. Ruth, determined to follow her own choice to stay with Naomi, despite counsel to the contrary and despite all common sense, establishes for Naomi a fullness in old age and for Jesus an ancestor who knows about God's sheltering wings. She brings into clear focus the God Jesus will call Abba, who figures so centrally in the Christian Lord's prayer. Bathsheba, who comes first to the sexual bed and then to the marriage bed of her adulterous king over the murdered corpse of her husband, occasions a *metanoia*, or change of heart, in the king, so that the whole idea and enactment of kingship alter in David, who is compelled to put religious devotion and penitence first. This also is to be fully realized in Christ, who takes on penitence for all our sins because, as he says, the first devotion is to love God with all our heart and mind and soul.

Looking at these female ancestors makes us turn around in our view of our religion and see that they bring essential new elements to its feminine components. We must cross borders that we have taken as clear and well defined and finished. Order and counterorder mix, and inexorably come together. Out of their apparent ambiguity a new order—what Jesus displays as New Being—arrives. Personal fulfillment and doing God's will not only mix, but the one becomes the path and the means for the breaking in of the other. Sometimes the personal brings the divine, sometimes the divine brings the filling out of the personal. In Jesus' lineage all parts flow together and no longer can be defined apart from one another.

These women all exhibit a commanding quality of mind: they combine a relentless logic with the capacity of the contemplative to take in what really is. These are two aspects of mind, or mental functioning, that we usually treat as opposites or, worse, as mutually exclusive. Tamar sees the customary route to conceiving a child in marriage closed to her. She sets aside male-imposed societal conventions to arrive at her own truth, which will turn out to be Yahweh's truth. She looks at other ways, unorthodox means; she fixes upon an unorthodox plan and goes to it with relentless logic to drive it to its conclusion. Rahab sizes up two opposing armies, two opposing faiths, with the logistics of a great tactician. She plots her battles: she not only seizes the stronger faith, but pours all of herself into it in recognition of the presence of the transcendent in it. In her bigger view, she sees the logic of what she must do and, even though it means treachery, proceeds with every determination to her goal. Ruth, from her clear view of the big welcoming God that Naomi worships, proceeds with inexorable logic to secure her future in Naomi's faith. We do not know, as I have emphasized as strongly as possible, about Bathsheba from her own point of view. She shows us starkly our centuries-old habit of seeing the female through a male's eyes. We do not know what she herself sees and contemplates. She personifies mystery, onto which David's seeing is projected. She is the inscrutability of nature, the fathomless beauty portrayed in countless paintings of the female body (upon which male purposes have been wrought). Bathsheba is what is contemplated in the mystery of woman and the sexuality she brings with her. David's life and relation to God and the life of his kingdom are all changed in a ruthlessly logical unfolding as a result of his taking her. So it is that all these female ancestors take risks, or occasion others to do so, and bring to our consciousness a mixture of contemplative gazing and relentless logic.

Although all of these women are mothers, none is noted for maternal feelings, and we do not associate Rahab with maternity despite the fact that Boaz is her son. Even Mary, Mother of God, is not exemplary of maternal ways of being-in-relation to her son, after the first archetypal image of the nursing couple. All are notable instead for the way they bring their lives to a boiling point for the birth events, for their free consenting to what happens to them. Not one of them blames anyone else. They fully accept and carry full responsibility for their own being. In this way the five can be called spiritual virgins, if not biological ones. All five are women who remain intact in their devotion to what moves from God into their own deeper Self and up to consciousness. They make themselves ready to let something pivotal and awesome occur in them, even if outside all conventional boundaries and laws and scandalous in society's view. They are not ruled by abstract ideas or ego purposes. They cannot be defined as father's daughters, obedient to culture, custom, law, or a paternal ethic. Nor can they be defined as mother's daughters, good girls occupied with mothering, with things of blood, milk, fertility. With the exception of Bathsheba, they are not defined either by their husbands or the sons they come by in such travail.

Bathsheba proves the exception. She is an unknown quantity, as I must keep emphasizing, not seen in the story from her own point of view. She remains all but voiceless about her desires for David, her guilt and grief over the deaths of her husband Uriah and her first-born baby, her gladness over her second-born son, Solomon, or her pleasure at being queen mother in Solomon's reign. We do not know how she feels about her own bewitching beauty or how she relates to its power. Bathsheba is most familiar as an example of what many twentieth-century women react against—being seen only through their effect on men, subsumed within male subjectivity and mute about their own. And yet Bathsheba is firmly included in Jesus' lineage. Why? Not only, I would suggest, for her revolutionary effect upon David and the relation of political and sexual power to devotion to God, but also because she exemplifies how the life of woman can be so taken up with conceiving, changing, influencing the lives of others, especially her mate and her offspring.

Bathsheba might be seen to represent this silent revolutionary power of women, which can be used up by others but which can also be, as it has been for millions of women, fulfilling and creative. A true creation occurs because of her. It is not so much associated with a sense of her, of her doing something; rather it is through her influence on another, as if she reaches right to the unconscious life of the other. In this experience women know in their bones the differences they have made in the lives of those they love. And they also know, in sad contrast, how this power can lay waste to a woman's sense of her own achievement, how she can be consumed by her caring for others and left with the feeling that no record remains of what she has accomplished.

What is startling about Bathsheba is that hers is the unabashed accomplishment of beauty and sexuality—not the work of mother, teacher, nurse, or wise guide. She is openly and altogether sexual—there, where she stands in the Tree of Jesse and of Jesus. And David does not blame her nor repudiate her after his crime is exposed and punished. He goes on relating to her sexually.

What stands out about Tamar, Rahab, Ruth, and Bathsheba (in her own odd way) is their untrammeled, savage, wily, virginal natures. The first three are virginal in being one in themselves, not defined by relationship with those outside themselves. Each is free in herself and free in relation to others. They do everything for their offspring or kin, as does Bathsheba finally, but they cannot be said to be possessed by their children or family. Bathsheba brings into this freedom a note of ambiguity. She lets herself be acted upon, drawing the king to her by the power of her beauty, allowing him to work upon her what will change him and her and her husband and the kingdom. Bathsheba is virginal in the sense that nature is, seemingly passive, empty, silently waiting to be acted upon and filled. Yet out of this virginal stillness comes all of life.

All four ancestresses know allegiance to the God who touches them in the particulars of their lives, bringing the holy, the transcendent, right into the midst of their most personal yearnings—Tamar's desire for a child, Rahab's craving for safety, Ruth's love of Naomi, Bathsheba's occasioning of her king's penitence. These women are chaste in the sense of putting first things first and remaining faithful to them. From such intact women comes the Son whose origin and purpose are transcendent, outside manmade customs, fulfilling the spirit of the law by breaking its letter. This is the God who changes a law-laden religion by creating a church in which all are made new, no longer simply Gentile or Jew, male or female, slave or free. [3]

These women bring with them the vital, deeply needed elements of the left-out feminine. It is as if the impulse to include the feminine begins on God's side, through these female ancestors from whom in time God will be born. They act as psychopomps, connecting a surface religion to the depth elements of sexuality and spirituality repressed and feared by so many. In Tamar we find dramatized the dread of woman, the primordial fear that to sleep with her is to be killed. In Bathsheba, we see the dread of the menstrual blood of women and the fear that intercourse with a woman can steal a man's powers to live and to fight. With Tamar, and with Ruth as well, though at a greater distance, we touch upon the incest taboo; with Rahab, treason; with Bathsheba, adultery; with Ruth again the far reaches of love between women. In all four we see deceit become a resource of devotion. In Bathsheba we see the enchantment a woman's beauty can work and the necessity of feminine mediation between the opposites of one man's deceit—David's—and another's unbending honor—Uriah's. With Tamar's, Rahab's, and Ruth's association to sacred prostitution, we see sexuality as congress with the divine. In Bathsheba we see the transforming effect of a man's image of woman on his whole life and work.

In all of these women, we find the closest association of sexuality and spirituality, something often deemphasized if not actually attacked in the teachings of our tradition. These women reconnect us with the instinctual basis of our faith, revealing it as a central resource, not something to be cast aside or triumphed over. They bequeath to Jesus, and through him to us, the seeds of woman as person and as believer. In his relations with women, Jesus redeems the female—she is no longer a being of dreaded sexuality or tainted blood, a being reduced to a natural force, identified only with fertility, blood, and milk. Jesus redeems woman from being seen only in terms of men's images of her. She is fully herself, to be judged, forgiven, blessed; to be used in parables to represent God's actions and to reveal God's truths; to be a loving follower, a beloved friend, a lover.

What blossoms in Mary is prefigured in the four female ancestors of Jesus: they are our intercessors. Standing on the borders of law and convention, they mediate new aspects of the God who is coming to be known to us and show us how we may respond in the fullest way to the Holy One who comes. Tamar intercedes for Judah, for him who kept his son away from her in fear of her deadly powers and who would condemn in her what he excused in himself. She shows us the grand motif of the trickster who does the wrong thing for the right reason. Rahab intercedes for family and kin. She shows us the frightening logic that leads us to take the grace that is offered us and makes secondary all other allegiances. She shows us the importance of that breadth of attitude that produces a subtlety and fullness of reaction to specific situations—with no generalizations, no sure-fire universal principles to direct behavior. Her God is not abstract but alive and responsive to us and to everything in us. We must be the same in relation to such a God.

Ruth intercedes for Naomi and Boaz and shows us a God with wings, a mother bird in whom we may trust and find refuge. This God acts in us when we are led to show others that same unbounding kindness and willingness to be for others. Bathsheba, by her effect on David, turns him from being the most powerful king in worldly terms to the most religious, thus showing us, in her psychological and spiritual directions, where we go wrong and what follows as a result. We go wrong when we worship the thing or person or quality that conveys the transcendent to us in place of the transcendent itself. We fall for substitutes, we take the messenger for the message and discard its sender. As a result, others, in no way involved with our mistakes, end up with the greatest suffering. Our blindness to the real thing fragments and kills others. The innocent suffer immeasurably. We must know that we are bound up in each other as we are in our dependence on God. Bathsheba plays the role in David's life that will bring this truth home to him and through his penitence to us.

In Jesus we see these seeds flower; we see Jesus bloom. It is he who says, following Tamar, that the person means more than the rule, and so we may, if necessary, pick corn or do anything else we must do on the Sabbath. Jesus says, following Rahab: I am coming, follow me, take what I bring you; leave me and you will be left. It is Jesus, again following Rahab, who spins in his parables attitudes of subtlety that penetrate to the core of every manner of concrete situation. It is Jesus, following Ruth, who recognizes the unbounding kindness and being-for-the-other in the woman who bathes his feet with her tears and wipes them with her hair. It is Jesus, following Bathsheba, who knows in his own blood that the innocent suffer unjustly and yet must offer up their suffering in penitence for the sins of the rest of us. It is Jesus, following Mary, who utterly consents to God acting through her body, who gives himself completely to God acting through his body for love of us while we are yet sinners.

NOTES

1. Some scholars think Luke traces Jesus' descent through Mary, presenting her as from the house of David (Luke 1:32), although that is not expressly stated. See J. D. Douglas, ed., *The New Bible Dictionary of the Christian Church* (London: Intervarsity Fellowship, 1962), p. 459; see also Raymond E. Brown, et al., eds., *Mary in the New Testament* (Philadelphia: Fortress Press, 1978), pp. 163 n. 371, 164 n. 372.

2. Marie-Louise von Franz, *Creation Myths* (Zurich: Spring Publications, 1972), p. 202. The term *collective unconscious*, coined by Jung, refers, as he says, to "all psychic contents that belong not to one individual but to many, i.e., to a society, a people, or to mankind in general. . . . [such as] general concepts of justice, the state, religion, science, etc., current among civilized man. It is not only concepts and ways of looking at things, however, . . . but also *feelings*. . . . not merely intellectual but emotional. . . . certain collective ideas . . . are bound up with collective feelings. This collective quality adheres not only to particular psychic elements or contents but to whole *functions*. . . . the feeling function as a whole can be collective, when it is identified with the general feeling and accords with general expectations. . . ." From C. G. Jung, *Psychological Types*, vol. 6 of the *Collected Works* (Princeton: Princeton University Press, 1971), par. 692.

3. Von Franz, *Creation Myths*, p. 202.

4. Ibid., p. 206.

5. Ibid., pp. 212–14.

6. See C. G. Jung, "Synchronicity: An Acausal Connecting Principle," in vol. 8 of the *Collected Works* (New York: Pantheon, 1960), par. 912, 923, 931, 948.

7. See Monica McGoldrick and Randy Gerson, *Genograms in Family Assessment* (New York: Norton, 1985).

8. All examples are taken from my practice as a psychoanalyst unless otherwise indicated, with gratitude to the persons who allowed me to use their material. This example also illustrates the powerful role nonhuman aspects of our environment play in our psychic life. See

Harold F. Searles, *The Nonhuman Environment* (New York: International Universities Press, 1960).

9. Raymond Brown notes that the New Testament genealogies bear a theological intention to establish Jesus as God's son and as savior to Gentile as well as Jew. See Raymond E. Brown, *The Birth of the Messiah* (New York: Doubleday, 1977), pp. 90–95; see also Raymond E. Brown, *A Coming Christ in Advent* (Collegeville, Minn.: Liturgical Press, 1988), chaps. 1 and 2.

10. See Ann Belford Ulanov, *The Feminine in Jungian Psychology and in Christian Theology* (Evanston, Ill.: Northwestern University Press, 1971), chap. 8. See also Ann Belford Ulanov, *Receiving Woman: Studies in the Psychology and Theology of the Feminine* (Philadelphia: Westminster, 1981), chap. 4; Ann Belford Ulanov, "Between Anxiety and Faith: The Role of the Feminine in Tillich's Theological Thought," in *Paul Tillich on Creativity*, ed. Jacquelyn Ann K. Kegley (New York: University Press of America, 1989).

11. For example, Jesus says to Martha, I am the resurrection and the life (John 11:25); he says to the Samaritan woman, I am the living water and the living spirit (John 4:13–15); it is to the Magdalene that he first appears resurrected (John 20:15–18).

12. Jung says of numbers: "There is something peculiar, one might even say mysterious about numbers. They have never been entirely robbed of their numinous aura. . . . Number helps more than anything else to bring order into the chaos of appearances. It is the predestined instrument for creating order, or for apprehending an already existing, but still unknown, regular arrangement or 'orderedness.' " Jung, "Synchronicity," in vol. 8 of the *Collected Works*, par. 870.

13. See Marie-Louise von Franz, *Number and Time: Reflections Leading Toward a Reunification of Depth Psychology and Physics* (Evanston, Ill.: Northwestern University Press, 1974), pp. 41–42, 60, 115–17.

14. See Jung, *Psychological Types*, vol. 6 of the *Collected Works*, par. 628–71. See also Edward F. Edinger, *Anatomy of the Psyche: Alchemical Symbolism in Psychotherapy* (LaSalle, Ill.: Open Court, 1985), pp. 188–89.

15. See C. G. Jung, *Psychology and Religion: West and East*, vol. 11 of the *Collected Works* (New York: Pantheon, 1958), par. 100ff., 245ff., 272f. See also J. E. Circlot, *A Dictionary of Symbols* (New York: Philosophical Library, 1962), p. 222; J. C. Cooper, *An Illustrated Encyclopedia of Traditional Symbols* (New York: Thames and Hudson, 1990), p. 115;

and *The Herder Symbol Dictionary* (Wilmette, Ill.: Chiron, 1986), p. 82.

16. For discussion of humans being the fourth in the Trinity, see Ann Belford Ulanov, *The Wisdom of the Psyche* (Cambridge, Mass.: Cowley Press, 1987), chap. 3.

17. See von Franz, *Number and Time*, pp. 65, 120. See also Cooper, *Encyclopedia of Traditional Symbols*, p. 116; Circlot, *Dictionary of Symbols*, p. 222; and *The Herder Symbol Dictionary*, pp. 77–78.

18. Von Franz, *Number and Time*, p. 123.

19. Jung, *Psychology and Religion*, vol. 11 of the *Collected Works*, par. 332.

20. See D. W. Winnicott, *Home Is Where We Start From*, ed. Clare Winnicot, Ray Shepherd, and Madeleine Davis (New York: W. W. Norton, 1986), p. 192.

21. A way to conceive of this female component psychologically is to draw on the different vocabularies of schools of depth psychology. Freud refers to the feminine component as part of our bisexuality; the object relations school of theorists, such as Harry Guntrip and D. W. Winnicott, refer to female elements of being; the Jung school uses the word *anima* to refer to the feminine in the male psyche and *animus* to refer to the masculine in the female psyche. Though differences exist among the theorists, all recognize that each of us is made up of aspects associated with each sex and gender. What stands out about Jesus is the depth and range of his access to the feminine mode of being, as illustrated in his free and varied relations to all kinds and all ages of women.

22. See C. G. Jung, "A Review of Complex Theory," in vol. 8 of the *Collected Works* (New York: Pantheon, 1960), pp. 92–107.

23. See Ann Belford Ulanov, "Picturing God," in *Picturing God* (Cambridge, Mass.: Cowley Press, 1986), pp. 164–84.

24. Ludwig Wittgenstein, *Philosophical Investigations* (Oxford: Blackwell, 1953), p. 223, cited by Gerard Radnitzsky, *Continental Schools of Metascience*, vol. 2 of *Contemporary Schools of Metascience* (Göteborg, Sweden: Akademiförlaget, 1968), p. 44 n. 58.

25. Radnitzsky, *Continental Schools*, p. 58.

26. For discussion of the kinds and importance of transference, see Ann Belford Ulanov, "Transference/Countertransference: A Jungian View" in *Jungian Analysis*, ed. Murray Stein (La Salle, Ill.: Open Court, 1982), pp. 68–86. A number of authors consider the application of depth psychology to Scripture. I include only a sampling. Many are Jungian, as that method lends itself particularly to this task

because it emphasizes the amplification of symbols to their fullest context. See Wayne G. Rollins, *Jung and the Bible* (Louisville: John Knox Press, 1983). See also Gerald H. Slusser, *From Jung to Jesus: Myth and Consciousness in the New Testament* (Louisville: John Knox Press, 1986); Edward F. Edinger, *The Bible and the Psyche: Individuation Symbolism in the Old Testament* (Toronto: Inner City Books, 1986); Edward F. Edinger, *The Christian Archetype: A Jungian Commentary on the Life of Christ* (Toronto: Inner City Books, 1987); Rivkah Schärf Kluger, *Psyche and Bible* (Zurich: Spring Publications, 1974); Erich Wellisch, *Isaac and Oedipus* (London: Routledge and Kegan Paul, 1954); Sharon MacIsaac, *Freud and Original Sin* (New York: Paulist Press, 1974).

27. Radnitzsky, *Continental Schools*, p. 51.

28. Ibid., p. 52.

29. Ibid., p. 50.

CHAPTER 2: TAMAR

1. *The Complete Bible, An American Translation*, trans. J. H. Powis Smith and Edgar J. Goodspeed (Chicago, Ill.: The University of Chicago Press, 1951). *The Anchor Bible* notes that the word *votary* is used when Judah returns asking for the woman to whom he promised the kid. Votaries came from the class of temple women employed for services connected with cult practices. They were not the priestesses, but they were not common harlots either. See *Genesis*, vol. 1 of *The Anchor Bible* (Garden City: Doubleday, 1964), pp. 299–300. *The Interpreter's Bible* comments that the author inserts the word *prostitute* (as distinct from common harlot), implying Judah's relation with her was more than a vulgar adventure, but had religious overtones even though that religion was abhorrent to Israel. See *Genesis*, vol. 1 of *The Interpreter's Bible* (New York: Abingdon, 1952), p. 758.

2. Rabbi Dr. H. Freedman, *Midrash Rabbah, Genesis*, 2 vols. (London: Socino Press, 1983), p. 796. Tamar was said to be the daughter of Shem, the son of Noah. The daughter of any priest if she plays the harlot is to be burned.

3. See *Interpreter's Bible, Genesis*, p. 758.

4. See *Anchor Bible, Genesis*, p. 300.

5. *Midrash Rabbah, Genesis*, pp. 796–97.

6. See Mary Hayter, *The New Eve in Christ* (Grand Rapids: Eerdmans, 1987), pp. 13–18, 27–28, 32, 35, 38, 40, 93; see also Phyllis Trible,

God and the Rhetoric of Sexuality (Philadelphia: Fortress Press, 1978), pp. 23 n. 5, 69, 139 n. 2.

7. For discussion of passion within permanence, see Ulanov, *The Feminine*, pp. 296–313.

8. See Winnicott, *Home Is Where We Start From*, p. 125. See also W. R. D. Fairbairn, *An Object Relations Theory of Personality* (New York: Basic Books, 1962), pp. 10–27, 265; Harry Guntrip, *Schizoid Phenomena, Object Relations and the Self* (New York: International Universities Press, 1969), pp. 39, 54, 74, 105–6; Melanie Klein, "Early Stages of the Oedipus Complex," in *Love, Guilt and Reparation and Other Works, 1921–1945* (New York: Delacorte Press, Seymour Lawrence, 1975), p. 190.

9. See Wolfgang Lederer, *The Fear of Women* (New York: Grune and Stratton, 1968), especially chap. 6, "A Snapping of Teeth," and chap. 19, "Envy and Loathing—The Patriarchal Revolt." See also Karen Horney, *Feminine Psychology* (New York: W. W. Norton, 1967), especially "The Dread of Woman" and "The Denial of the Vagina," pp. 133–47, 147–62; Melanie Klein, "Envy and Gratitude" in *Envy and Gratitude and Other Works 1946–1963* (New York: Delacorte Press, Seymour Lawrence, 1975), p. 201; Otto Rank, "Feminine Psychology and Masculine Ideology" in *Beyond Psychology* (New York: Dover, 1941). We can appreciate the profundity of Scripture, which touches on this primordial theme that is examined again in the twentieth century by depth psychology. For a discussion of the idea that one result of the Fall is the polarization of the sexes that manifests through contempt for the female, see Ulanov, *The Feminine*, pp. 293–313.

10. See Mary Callaway, *Sing, O Barren One: A Study in Comparative Midrash*, SBL Series no. 91 (Atlanta: Scholar's Press, 1980), p. 13ff. See also C. G. Jung, "Psychological Aspects of the Mother Archetype," in vol. 9:1 of the *Collected Works* (New York: Pantheon, 1959), par. 148–98.

11. See *Anchor Bible, Genesis*, p. 299; see also *Interpreter's Bible, Genesis*, p. 758.

12. For discussion of the range of goddesses connected with the cult, see Nancy Qualls-Corbett, *The Sacred Prostitute: Eternal Aspect of the Feminine* (Toronto: Inner City Books, 1988), chap. 1, and pp. 34–85.

13. Ibid., p. 62.

14. Ibid., pp. 39, 74–78.

15. For discussion of this tale and its psychological interpretation, see Ann and Barry Ulanov, *The Witch and the Clown: Two Archetypes of Human Sexuality* (Wilmette, Ill.: Chiron, 1987), chap. 3.

16. Jung writes, "The overwhelming majority of men on the present cultural level never advance beyond the maternal significance of woman, and this is the reason why the anima seldom develops beyond the infantile, primitive level of the prostitute. Consequently prostitution is one of the main by-products of civilized marriage." C. G. Jung, "Mind and Earth," in vol. 10 of the *Collected Works* (New York: Pantheon, 1964), par. 76.

17. For discussion of reaching the transcendent through the passionate, committed personal relationship, see Ulanov, *The Feminine*, p. 431.

18. Edinger, *Christian Archetype*, p. 28.

19. For discussion of psychological virginity, see M. Esther Harding, *Women's Mysteries: Ancient and Modern* (New York: Longman's, Green, 1985), chap. 13.

20. For discussion of the trickster motif, see C. G. Jung, "On the Psychology of the Trickster-Figure," in vol. 9:1 of the *Collected Works* (New York: Pantheon, 1959), par. 456–88.

21. See James G. Williams, *Women Recounted: Narrative Thinking and the God of Israel* (Sheffield, England: Almond Press, 1982), pp. 93–102. See also J. M. Sasson, *Ruth* (Baltimore: Johns Hopkins, 1979), p. 232.

CHAPTER 3: RAHAB

1. See Cooper, *Encyclopedia of Traditional Symbols*, pp. 40–41; see also *Herder Dictionary of Symbols*, p. 157.

2. For discussion of a woman's task of harnessing masculine energies, see A. and B. Ulanov, "The Hag," in *The Witch and the Clown*, chaps. 4–7.

3. *Midrash Rabbah, Ruth*, trans. Rabbi Dr. L. Rabinowitz (London: Socino Press, 1983), pp. 23–24.

4. For discussion of the multiple roles of intercession, especially as it affects inner parts of ourselves as well as others in our community, see Ann and Barry Ulanov, *Religion and the Unconscious* (Philadelphia: Westminster Press, 1975), chap. 11; see also Ann and Barry Ulanov, *Primary Speech: A Psychology of Prayer* (Louisville: John Knox Press, 1983), chap. 9.

5. For discussion of corresponding with grace, see Ann and Barry Ulanov, *Cinderella and Her Sisters: The Envied and the Envying* (Philadelphia: Westminster, 1983), 147–53.

6. See Jung, *Psychology and Religion*, vol. 11 of the *Collected Works*, par. 167. See also 1 John 4:1–3; Teresa of Avila, *The Interior Castle*, in vol. 2 of *The Complete Works of St. Teresa* (New York: Sheed and Ward, 1957), pp. 4, 7, 346.

7. *Midrash Rabbah, Ruth*, p. 24.

8. Ibid., p. 25.

9. Cooper, *Encyclopedia of Traditional Symbols*, p. 156.

10. *Herder Symbol Dictionary*, p. 55. For discussion of the mixtures of bad and good that are found in the "matriarchal superego" in contrast to the "patriarchal superego," see A. and B. Ulanov, *Religion and the Unconscious*, pp. 150–57.

11. Circlot, *Dictionary of Symbols*, p. 290.

12. Cooper, *Encyclopedia of Traditional Symbols*, p. 156.

13. For a discussion of spinning and subtlety of attitude in relation to fairy tales, see Marie-Louise von Franz, *The Feminine in Fairy Tales* (New York: Spring Publications, 1972), p. 192ff.

14. For further discussion of praying, see A. and B. Ulanov, *Primary Speech*.

15. For discussion of the notion of psychological virginity, see John Layard, *The Virgin Archetype* (Dallas: Spring Publications, 1972).

16. Douglas, *New Bible Dictionary*, p. 1074.

17. *Joshua*, vol. 2 of *The Interpreter's Bible* (New York: Abingdon, 1953), p. 561.

CHAPTER 4: RUTH

1. *The Interpreter's Bible, Ruth*, p. 837. The symbolism of the bee is apt here. The Queen Bee represents the Great Mother with her priestesses around her. Bees were believed to be parthogenic, hence symbolizing virginity. They represent the spirit world, rebirth, immortality. See Cooper, *Encyclopedia of Traditional Symbols*, p. 19. Jung notes that "in Tantric yoga an 'indistinct hum of swarms of love-mad bees' proceeds from the slumbering Shakti." Mary is also associated with bees. See C. G. Jung, "The Psychological Aspects of the Kore," in vol. 9:1 of the *Collected Works* (New York: Pantheon, 1959), p. 185n. Though having only a sympathetic nervous system, bees nevertheless display incredibly organized behavior. They have been taken to symbolize, therefore, unconscious order or harmony outside of rational organization. Jung makes an interesting comment about the suprapersonal, collective aspects of communication

through the sympathetic nervous system, as instanced here by the gathering of women around Naomi:

> The sympathetic nervous system is an exceedingly emotional centre, and it rules to a great extent the emotional part of our psychology, not the mental part. . . . [T]he word 'sympathetic' . . . comes from the Greek word meaning to suffer, to feel compassion, to feel together with, so it has the connotation of connection of relatedness. . . . [T]he sympathetic emotion has an almost cosmic character, as if you were suffering with man, as if you were connected to the whole world, your whole nation. . . . It has nothing to do with individuation, but it has to do with the whole history of man, including animals; it is collective, out of yourself, as if a strange thing had taken possession of you.

From C. G. Jung, *Dream Analysis: Notes of the Seminars Given in 1928–1930*, ed. William McGuire (Princeton: Princeton University Press, 1984), p. 335.

2. Williams, *Women Recounted*, p. 107.

3. H. Yechezkel Kluger, "Ruth: A Contribution to the Development of the Feminine in the Old Testament," *Spring 1957* (New York: The Analytical Psychology Club of New York, 1957), pp. 52–86. I am indebted to this reading of Ruth, with its emphasis on recovering the neglected feminine.

4. See, for example, Marie-Louise von Franz's remarks in *Individuation in Fairy Tales* (Zurich: Spring Publications, 1977), p. 105:

> I have said to Dr. Jung that sometimes it seemed to me as if Jungian psychology were a highly dangerous poison, the poison of truth. He agreed that to take it up and then leave it again is absolutely destructive poison. Once one has had enough realization of what goes on inside one and of what it is all about, then one can only escape at the price of becoming highly neurotic.

Saint Teresa of Avila says something similar: that we should not start a life of prayer and then stop it. It would be better not to have started it because, once started, prayer is like climbing a ladder. When you break it off, you have already begun to climb up the rungs and thus fall from a greater height with more likelihood of injuring yourself. See Teresa of Avila, *Interior Castle*, pp. 244–46.

5. See Kluger, *Ruth*, pp. 56–57, for discussion of the relevance to Ruth of the Adonis-Tammuz myths.

6. Williams, *Women Recounted*, p. 109.

7. See D. R. G. Beattie, "Jewish Exegesis of the Book of Ruth," *Journal for the Study of the Old Testament*, Supplement Series 2 (Sheffield, England: University of Sheffield, Department of Biblical Studies, 1977), p. 66.

8. For discussion of Ruth's radical courage, see Trible, *God and the Rhetoric of Sexuality* (Philadelphia: Fortress Press, 1978), chap. 6.

9. See John Craghan, *Esther, Judith, Tobit, Jonah, Ruth* (Wilmington, Del.: Michael Glazier, 1982), p. 210. See also Louis Ginzberg, *The Legends of the Jews*, vol. 4 (Philadelphia: Jewish Publication Society of America, 1982), p. 33; Douglas, *New Bible Dictionary*, p. 1109; and *Interpreter's Bible, Ruth*, p. 851.

10. See Trible, *God and the Rhetoric of Sexuality*, p. 172. See also Craghan, *Esther, Judith*, p. 56.

11. Kluger, *Ruth*, p. 58.

12. Ibid., p. 74.

13. Ginzberg, *Legends of the Jews*, p. 31.

14. See Ulanov, *Receiving Woman*, pp. 76–80.

15. See Sasson, *Ruth*, p. 192.

16. Kluger, *Ruth*, p. 65.

17. For discussion of the profundity of woman's wiles, see Ulanov, *Wisdom of the Psyche*, chap. 3.

18. *Interpreter's Bible, Ruth*, p. 844.

19. Ibid., p. 846. See also Beattie, "Jewish Exegesis," p. 121.

20. For discussion, see Sasson, *Ruth*, pp. 247–48.

21. For discussion of psychological and spiritual virginity, see Layard, *Virgin Archetypes*, pp. 288–97.

22. See, for example, Anthony Trollope, *The American Senator* (London: Oxford University Press, 1931); see also Trollope's *Lady Anna* (London: Oxford University Press, 1931) and *The Kelleys and the O'Kelleys* (London: Oxford University Press, 1951).

23. *Midrash Rabbah, Ruth*, p. 40.

24. See Williams, *Women Recounted*, p. 120.

25. Ginzberg, *Legends of the Jews*, p. 33.

26. For discussion of polarization between the sexes, see Ulanov, *The Feminine*, pp. 296–303.

27. See Janine Chasseguet-Smirgel, *Creativity and Perversion* (New York: W. W. Norton, 1985), pp. 146–48, 154; see also her *Sexuality and the Mind: The Role of the Father and the Mother in the Psyche* (New York: New York Universities Press, 1986), p. 77.

28. See Judith L. Herman, *Father-Daughter Incest* (Cambridge: Harvard University Press, 1981); see also her *Trauma and Recovery* (New York: Basic Books, 1992).

29. *The Zohar*, trans. H. Sperling and M. Simon, 5 vols. (London: Socino Press, 1931–1934), vol. 2, p. 218, cited by Kluger, *Ruth*, p. 73.

30. See C. G. Jung, "Some Aspects of Modern Psychotherapy," in vol. 16 of the *Collected Works* (New York: Pantheon, 1954), par. 55–56.

31. See Ulanov, "Transference/Countertransference" in *Jungian Analysis*, p. 76.

32. See Ann and Barry Ulanov, *Anima and Animus: Archetypes of Transformation*, forthcoming.

33. See C. G. Jung, "Psychology of the Transference," in vol. 16 of the *Collected Works* (New York: Pantheon, 1954), par. 458.

34. Ibid., par. 460.

35. See Sasson, *Ruth*, p. 194; see also Williams, *Women Recounted*, p. 121.

36. Kluger, *Ruth*, p. 80.

37. Ibid.

38. See C. G. Jung, "The Shadow" in vol. 9:2 of the *Collected Works* (New York: Pantheon, 1959), par. 13–19; see also Joseph L. Henderson, *Shadow and Self: Selected Papers in Analytical Psychology* (Wilmette, Ill.: Chiron, 1990).

39. See Cooper, *Encyclopedia of Traditional Symbols*, p. 144; see also *Herder Symbol Dictionary*, p. 173.

40. *Midrash Rabbah, Ruth*, p. 33, describes Naomi: "She was left the remnants of remnants." See also Johanna W. H. Bos, *Ruth, Esther, Jonah* (Atlanta: John Knox Press, 1986), p. 20. See also Trible, *God and the Rhetoric of Sexuality*, p. 173: "One female has chosen another female in a world where life depends on men." Trible also says that throughout Ruth is the "defier of custom, the maker of decisions, and the worker of salvation" (p. 184), and of Naomi and Ruth: "Altogether they are women in culture, women against culture, and women transforming culture" (p. 196).

41. Williams, *Recounting Women*, p. 106: "Ruth has come to Yahweh as to a mother." See also Bos, *Ruth, Esther*, p. 28, and *Midrash Rabbah, Ruth*, p. 61. The following psalms cite God as if having wings: Pss. 17:8, 36:7, 57:2, 61:4, 91:4.

42. See Craghan, *Esther*, p. 198.

43. *Zohar Ruth*, cited by Kluger, *Ruth*, p. 74.

44. *Midrash Rabbah, Ruth*, p. 36.

CHAPTER 5: BATHSHEBA

1. For a fascinating discussion of this point, see A. R. Pope, "The Eros Aspect of the Eye" (Küsnacht: C. G. Jung Institute Zurich, Kleine Schriften, 1968).

2. Ibid., p. 21.

3. For discussion of the menstrual taboo and fear of it, as well as its psychological meaning, see Ulanov, *The Feminine*, pp. 175–76, 183. See also Harding, *Women's Mysteries*, chaps. 5 and 6; Lederer, *Fear of the Female*, chaps. 5 and 7; Louis Finkelstein, ed., *The Jews and Their History, Culture and Religion* (New York: Harper, 1960); and Penelope Shuttle and Peter Redgrove, *The Wise Wound* (New York: Richard Marek Publishers, 1978).

4. For study of the male's bewitchment, see A. and B. Ulanov, *Witch and the Clown*, chaps. 3 and 8. See also Marie-Louise von Franz, *Apuleius' Golden Ass* (New York: Spring Publications, 1970).

5. Elizabeth Längesser, *The Quest* (New York: Knopf, 1953), pp. 149–51.

6. See Susan R. Suleiman, ed., *The Female Body in Western Culture* (Cambridge: Harvard University Press, 1986). See also Thomas B. Hess and Linda Nochlin, eds., *Woman as Sex-Object* (New York: Art News Annual 38, 1972).

7. For discussion of an example of voyeurism, see A. and B. Ulanov, *Witch and the Clown*, p. 176.

8. Pope, "Eros Aspect," pp. 24–25. Seeing as eating can also serve as a factor in eating disorders, as well as in religious aspects of fasting. See Caroline W. Bynum, *Holy Feast and Holy Food* (Berkeley: University of California Press, 1987). See also Judith Van Herik, "Simone Weil's Religious Imagery: How Looking Becomes Eating" in *Immaculate and Powerful: The Female in Sacred Image and Social Reality*, ed. Clarissa W. Atkinson, Constance H. Buchanan, and Margaret Miles (Boston: Beacon Press, 1985).

9. For discussion of psychological projection and projective identification, see Ulanov, *Receiving Woman*, chap. 3; for application of these ideas to the afterlife, see Ulanov, "Heaven and Hell" in *Picturing God*. See also Melanie Klein, "Notes on Some Schizoid Mechanisms (1946)," in *Envy and Gratitude*, pp. 1–25.

10. For discussion of this whole phenomenon of the anima woman, see C. G. Jung, "Concerning the Archetypes, with Special Reference to

the Anima Concept" in vol. 9:1 of the *Collected Works* (New York: Pantheon, 1959), par. 111–47. See also M. Esther Harding, *The Way of All Women* (New York: Putnam, 1970), chap. 1, and Ulanov, *The Feminine*, pp. 252–53, 256.

11. Pope, "Eros Aspect," p. 22.

12. For discussion of this entry into the soul through the feminine, see Ulanov, *Wisdom of the Psyche*, pp. 97–99. For discussion of Jung's notion of the Self, see C. G. Jung, *Mysterium Coniunctionis*, in vol. 14 of the *Collected Works* (New York: Pantheon, 1963), par. 4, 103, 133, 145, 176, 181, 498, 704.

13. Pope, in *Eros Aspect*, p. 6, comments: "The similarity in form between the eye and the vulva may be connected with this sexual significance of the eye. . . . Jung refers to this similarity, when Indra is covered with eyes instead of vulvae as punishment for blasphemy. Perhaps the vulva could be replaced by the eye without loss in Indra's case, meaning that the vulva has a 'seeing' aspect represented by the eye. In other words, Eros has a seeing quality." For discussion of the sexual intent in the violent crime of rape, see Barry Ulanov, "The Rages of Sin," *Union Seminary Quarterly Review*, vol. 44, nos. 1–2 (1990).

14. See Jacob Boehme, *The Way to Christ* (New York: Paulist Press, 1978), pp. 44, 154, 249. For clinical examples of the dilemma of a man caught between two women, see Ann Belford Ulanov, "Disguises of the Anima," in *Gender and Soul in Psychotherapy*, ed. Nathan Schwartz-Salant and Murray Stein (Wilmette, Ill.: Chiron Clinical Series, 1992).

15. For discussion of this conversation, see A. and B. Ulanov, "Intercession," in *Religion and the Unconscious*, chap. 11. Jung discusses the enlivening nature of these conversations in the idea of the "subtle body"; see C. G. Jung, *Alchemical Studies*, in vol. 13 of the *Collected Works* (Princeton: Princeton University Press, 1967), p. 104 n. 8, par. 213. Object relations theorists discuss the place of these conversations as "intrasubjective space." See Christopher Bollas, "Off the Wall," in *Forces of Destiny: Psychoanalysis and Human Idiom* (London: Free Association Press, 1991), pp. 52–53.

16. Cited in Jung, *Psychology and Religion*, in vol. 11 of the *Collected Works*, par. 133.

17. For discussion of this taboo of intercourse when a soldier is consecrated to battle, see *Interpreter's Bible, 2 Samuel*, vol. 2 (New York: Abingdon, 1953), p. 1100.

18. See C. G. Jung, *Aion*, in vol. 9:2 of the *Collected Works*, par. 13–14. See also Ulanov, "The Psychological Reality of the Demonic," in *Picturing God*.

19. See Paul Ricoeur, *The Symbolism of Evil* (New York: Harper and Row, 1967), pp. 33–40.

20. Ginzberg, *The Legends of the Jews*, p. 103. See also Edith Deen, *All the Women of the Bible* (New York: Harper, 1955), p. 113.

21. Ginzberg, *The Legends of the Jews*, p. 103.

CHAPTER 6: CONCLUSION

1. Brown, *Birth of the Messiah*, pp. 71–74, 90–95. See also F. Spitta, "Die Frauen in der Genealogie Jesu bei Matthaus," *Zeitschrift fur Wissenschaftliche Theologie* 54, (1912): 1–8; and Franz Schnider and Werner Stenger, "Die Frauen im Stammbaum Jesu nach Mattaus, Strukturale Beobachtungen zu Mt. 1–17," *Studien zum Neuen Testament* (New York: E. J. Brill, 1990).

2. See A. and B. Ulanov, *Witch and the Clown*, chap. 2.

3. See J. Louis Martyn, "Covenant, Christ, and Church in Galatians," Clark Lectures, Duke University, 9 April 1992.

APPENDIX

The following excerpts are from the New Revised Standard Version of the Bible.

THE GENEALOGY OF MATTHEW

MATTHEW 1:2–7

1 An account of the genealogy of Jesus the Messiah, the son of David, the son of Abraham.

2 Abraham was the father of Isaac, and Isaac the father of Jacob, and Jacob the father of Judah and his brothers, ³and Judah the father of Perez and Zerah by Tamar, and Perez the father of Hezron, and Hezron the father of Aram, ⁴and Aram the father of Aminadab, and Aminadab the father of Nahshon, and Nahshon the father of Salmon, ⁵and Salmon the father of Boaz by Rahab, and Boaz the father of Obed by Ruth, and Obed the father of Jesse, ⁶and Jesse the father of King David.

And David was the father of Solomon by the wife of Uriah, ⁷and Solomon the father of Rehoboam, and Rehoboam the father of Abijah, and Abijah the father of Asaph, ⁸and Asaph the father of Jehoshaphat, and Jehoshaphat the father of Joram, and Joram the father of Uzziah, ⁹and Uzziah the father of Jotham, and Jotham the father of Ahaz, and Ahaz the father of Hezekiah, ¹⁰and Hezekiah the father of Manasseh, and Manasseh the father of Amos, and Amos the father of Josiah, ¹¹and Josiah the father of Jechoniah and his brothers, at the time of the deportation to Babylon.

12 And after the deportation to Babylon: Jechoniah was the father of Salathiel, and Salathiel the father of Zerubbabel, ¹³and Zerubbabel the father of Abiud, and Abiud the father of Eliakim, and Eliakim the father of Azor, ¹⁴and Azor the father of Zadok, and Zadok the father of Achim, and Achim the father of Eliud, ¹⁵and Eliud the father of Eleazar, and Eleazar the father of Matthan, and Matthan the father of Jacob, ¹⁶and Jacob the father of Joseph the husband of Mary, of whom Jesus was born, who is called the Messiah.

17 So all the generations from Abraham to David are fourteen generations; and from David to the deportation to Babylon, fourteen generations; and from the deportation to Babylon to the Messiah, fourteen generations.

The Story of Tamar

GENESIS 38

1   It happened at that time that Judah went down from his brothers and settled near a certain Adullamite whose name was Hirah. ²There Judah saw the daughter of a certain Canaanite whose name was Shua; he married her and went in to her. ³She conceived and bore a son; and he named him Er. ⁴Again she conceived and bore a son whom she named Onan. ⁵Yet again she bore a son, and she named him Shelah. She was in Chezib when she bore him. ⁶Judah took a wife for Er his firstborn; her name was Tamar. ⁷But Er, Judah's firstborn, was wicked in the sight of the Lord, and the Lord put him to death. ⁸Then Judah said to Onan, "Go in to your brother's wife and perform the duty of a brother-in-law to her; raise up offspring for your brother." ⁹But since Onan knew that the offspring would not be his, he spilled his semen on the ground whenever he went in to his brother's wife, so that he would not give offspring to his brother. ¹⁰What he did was displeasing in the sight of the Lord, and he put him to death also. ¹¹Then Judah said to his daughter-in-law Tamar, "Remain a widow in your father's house until my son Shelah grows up"—for he feared that he too would die, like his brothers. So Tamar went to live in her father's house.

12 In course of time the wife of Judah, Shua's daughter, died; when Judah's time of mourning was over, he went up to Timnah to his sheepshearers, he and his friend Hirah the Adullamite. ¹³When Tamar was told, "Your father-in-law is going up to Timnah to shear his sheep," ¹⁴she put off her widow's garments, put on a veil, wrapped herself up, and sat down at the entrance to Enaim, which is on the road to Timnah. She saw that Shelah was grown up, yet she had not been given to him in marriage. ¹⁵When Judah saw her, he thought her to be a prostitute, for she had covered her face. ¹⁶He went over to her at the road side, and said, "Come, let me come in to you," for he did not know that she was his daughter-in-law. She said, "What will you give me, that you may come in to me?" ¹⁷He answered, "I will send you a kid from the flock." And she said, "Only if you give me a pledge, until you send it." ¹⁸He said, "What pledge shall I give you?" She replied, "Your signet and your cord, and the staff that is in your hand." So he gave them to her, and went in to her, and she conceived by him. ¹⁹Then she got up and went away, and taking off her veil she put on the garments of her widowhood.

20   When Judah sent the kid by his friend the Adullamite, to recover the pledge from the woman, he could not find her. ²¹He asked the townspeople, "Where is the temple prostitute who was at Enaim by the wayside?" But they said, "No prostitute has been here." ²²So he returned to Judah, and said, "I have not found her; moreover the townspeople said, 'No prostitute has been here.' " ²³Judah replied, "Let her keep the things as her own, otherwise we will be laughed at; you see, I sent this kid, and you could not find her."

24   About three months later Judah was told, "Your daughter-in-law Tamar has played the whore; moreover she is pregnant as a result of whoredom." And Judah said, "Bring her out, and let her be burned." ²⁵As she was being brought out, she sent word to her father-in-law, "It was the owner of these who made me pregnant." And she said, "Take note, please, whose these are, the signet and the cord and the staff." ²⁶Then Judah acknowledged them and said, "She is more in the right than I, since I did not give her to my son Shelah." And he did not lie with her again.

27   When the time of her delivery came, there were twins in her womb. ²⁸While she was in labor, one put out a hand; and the midwife took and bound on his hand a crimson thread, saying, "This one came out first." ²⁹But just then he drew back his hand, and out came his brother; and she said, "What a breach you have made for yourself!" Therefore he was named Perez. ³⁰Afterward his brother came out with the crimson on his hand; and he was named Zerah.

THE STORY OF RAHAB

JOSHUA 2

1   Then Joshua son of Nun sent two men secretly from Shittim as spies, saying, "Go, view the land, especially Jericho." So they went, and entered the house of a prostitute whose name was Rahab, and spent the night there. ²The king of Jericho was told, "Some Israelites have come here tonight to search out the land." ³Then the king of Jericho sent orders to Rahab, "Bring out the men who have come to you, who entered your house, for they have come only to search out the whole land." ⁴But the woman took the two men and hid them. Then she said, "True, the men came to me, but I did not know where they came from. ⁵And when it was time to close the gate at dark, the men went out. Where the men went I do not know. Pursue them quickly, for

you can overtake them." ⁶She had, however, brought them up to the roof and hidden them with the stalks of flax that she had laid out on the roof. ⁷So the men pursued them on the way to the Jordan as far as the fords. As soon as the pursuers had gone out, the gate was shut.

8 Before they went to sleep, she came up to them on the roof ⁹and said to the men: "I know that the Lord has given you the land, and that dread of you has fallen on us, and that all the inhabitants of the land melt in fear before you. ¹⁰For we have heard how the Lord dried up the water of the Red Sea before you when you came out of Egypt, and what you did to the two kings of the Amorites that were beyond the Jordan, to Sihon and Og, whom you utterly destroyed. ¹¹As soon as we heard it, our hearts melted, and there was no courage left in any of us because of you. The Lord your God is indeed God in heaven above and on earth below. ¹²Now then, since I have dealt kindly with you, swear to me by the Lord that you in turn will deal kindly with my family. Give me a sign of good faith ¹³that you will spare my father and mother, my brothers and sisters, and all who belong to them, and deliver our lives from death." ¹⁴The men said to her, "Our life for yours! If you do not tell this business of ours, then we will deal kindly and faithfully with you when the Lord gives us the land."

15 Then she let them down by a rope through the window, for her house was on the outer side of the city wall and she resided within the wall itself. ¹⁶She said to them, "Go toward the hill country, so that the pursuers may not come upon you. Hide yourselves there three days, until the pursuers have returned; then afterward you may go your way." ¹⁷The men said to her, "We will be released from this oath that you have made us swear to you ¹⁸if we invade the land and you do not tie this crimson cord in the window through which you let us down, and you do not gather into your house your father and mother, your brothers, and all your family. ¹⁹If any of you go out of the doors of your house into the street, they shall be responsible for their own death, and we shall be innocent; but if a hand is laid upon any who are with you in the house, we shall bear the responsibility for their death. ²⁰But if you tell this business of ours, then we shall be released from this oath that you made us swear to you." ²¹She said, "According to your words, so be it." She sent them away and they departed. Then she tied the crimson cord in the window.

22 They departed and went into the hill country and stayed there three days, until the pursuers returned. The pursuers had searched all along the way and found nothing. ²³Then the two men came down again from the hill country. They crossed over, came to Joshua son of Nun, and told him all that had happened to them. ²⁴They said to Joshua, "Truly the Lord has given all the land into our hands; moreover all the inhabitants of the land melt in fear before us."

THE STORY OF RUTH

RUTH 1:1–6

1 In the days when the judges ruled, there was a famine in the land, and a certain man of Bethlehem in Judah went to live in the country of Moab, he and his wife and two sons. ²The name of the man was Elimelech and the name of his wife Naomi, and the names of his two sons were Mahlon and Chilion; they were Ephrathites from Bethlehem in Judah. They went into the country of Moab and remained there. ³But Elimelech, the husband of Naomi, died, and she was left with her two sons. ⁴These took Moabite wives; the name of the one was Orpah and the name of the other Ruth. When they had lived there about ten years, ⁵both Mahlon and Chilion also died, so that the woman was left without her two sons and her husband.

6 Then she started to return with her daughters-in-law from the country of Moab, for she had heard in the country of Moab that the Lord had considered his people and given them food.

1:8–11

⁸But Naomi said to her two daughters-in-law, "Go back each of you to your mother's house. May the Lord deal kindly with you, as you have dealt with the dead and with me. ⁹The Lord grant that you may find security, each of you in the house of your husband." Then she kissed them, and they wept aloud. ¹⁰They said to her, "No, we will return with you to your people." ¹¹But Naomi said, "Turn back, my daughters, why will you go with me? Do I still have sons in my womb that they may become your husbands?

1:13–21

No, my daughters, it has been far more bitter for me than for you, because the hand of the Lord has turned against me."

¹⁴Then they wept aloud again. Orpah kissed her mother-in-law, but Ruth clung to her.

15 So she said, "See, your sister-in-law has gone back to her people and to her gods; return after your sister-in-law." ¹⁶But Ruth said, "Do not press me to leave you
or to turn back from following you!
Where you go, I will go;
Where you lodge, I will lodge;
your people shall be my people,
and your God my God.

17 Where you die, I will die—
there will I be buried.
May the Lord do thus and so to me,
and more as well,
if even death parts me from you!"
¹⁸When Naomi saw that she was determined to go with her, she said no more to her.

19 So the two of them went on until they came to Bethlehem. When they came to Bethlehem, the whole town was stirred because of them; and the women said, "Is this Naomi?" ²⁰She said to them,
"Call me no longer Naomi,
call me Mara,
for the Almighty has dealt bitterly with me.

21 I went away full,
but the Lord has brought me back empty;
why call me Naomi
when the Lord has dealt harshly with me,
and the Almighty has brought calamity upon me?"

1:22–2:12
They came to Bethlehem at the beginning of the barley harvest.

2 Now Naomi had a kinsman on her husband's side, a prominent rich man, of the family of Elimelech, whose name was Boaz. ²And Ruth the Moabite said to Naomi, "Let me go to the field and glean among the ears of grain, behind someone in whose sight I may find favor." She said to her, "Go, my daughter." ³So she went. She came and gleaned in the field behind the reapers, As it happened, she came to the part of the field belonging to Boaz, who was of the family of Elimelech. ⁴Just then Boaz came from Bethlehem. He said to the reapers, "The Lord be with you." They answered, "The Lord bless you." ⁵Then Boaz said

to his servant who was in charge of the reapers, "To whom does this young woman belong?" ⁶The servant who was in charge of the reapers answered, "She is the Moabite who came back with Naomi from the country of Moab. ⁷She said, 'Please, let me glean and gather among the sheaves behind the reapers.' So she came, and she has been on her feet from early this morning until now, without resting even for a moment."

8 Then Boaz said to Ruth, "Now listen, my daughter, do not go to glean in another field or leave this one, but keep close to my young women. ⁹Keep your eyes on the field that is being reaped, and follow behind them. I have ordered the young men not to bother you. If you get thirsty, go to the vessels and drink from what the young men have drawn." ¹⁰Then she fell prostrate, with her face to the ground, and said to him, "Why have I found favor in your sight, that you should take notice of me, when I am a foreigner?" ¹¹But Boaz answered her, "All that you have done for your mother-in-law since the death of your husband has been fully told me, and how you left your father and mother and your native land and came to a people that you did not know before. ¹²May the Lord reward you for your deeds, and may you have a full reward from the Lord, the God of Israel, under whose wings you have come for refuge!"

2:19–21

So she told her mother-in-law with whom she had worked, and said, "The name of the man with whom I worked today is Boaz." ²⁰Then Naomi said to her daughter-in-law, "Blessed be he by the Lord, whose kindness has not forsaken the living or the dead!" Naomi also said to her, "The man is a relative of ours, one of our nearest kin." ²¹Then Ruth the Moabite said, "He even said to me, 'Stay close by my servants, until they have finished all my harvest.' "

3:1–17

1 Naomi her mother-in-law said to her, "My daughter, I need to seek some security for you, so that it may be well with you. ²Now here is our kinsman Boaz, with whose young women you have been working. See, he is winnowing barley tonight at the threshing floor. ³Now wash and anoint yourself, and put on your best clothes and go down to the threshing floor; but do not make yourself known to the man until he has finished eating and drinking. ⁴When he lies down, observe the place where he lies;

then, go and uncover his feet and lie down; and he will tell you what to do." ⁵She said to her, "All that you tell me I will do."

6 So she went down to the threshing floor and did just as her mother-in-law had instructed her. ⁷When Boaz had eaten and drunk, and he was in a contented mood, he went to lie down at the end of the heap of grain. Then she came stealthily and uncovered his feet, and lay down. ⁸At midnight the man was startled, and turned over, and there, lying at his feet, was a woman! ⁹He said, "Who are you?" And she answered, "I am Ruth, your servant; spread your cloak over your servant, for you are next-of-kin." ¹⁰He said, "May you be blessed by the Lord, my daughter; this last instance of your loyalty is better than the first; you have not gone after young men, whether poor or rich. ¹¹And now, my daughter, do not be afraid, I will do for you all that you ask, for all the assembly of my people know that you are a worthy woman. ¹²But now, though it is true that I am a near kinsman, there is another kinsman more closely related than I. ¹³Remain this night, and in the morning, if he will act as next-of-kin for you, good; let him do it. If he is not willing to act as next-of-kin for you, then, as the Lord lives, I will act as next-of-kin for you. Lie down until the morning."

14 So she lay at his feet until morning, but got up before one person could recognize another; for he said, "It must not be known that the woman came to the threshing floor." ¹⁵Then he said, "Bring the cloak you are wearing and hold it out." So she held it, and he measured out six measures of barley, and put it on her back; then he went into the city. ¹⁶She came to her mother-in-law, who said, "How did things go with you, my daughter?" Then she told her all that the man had done for her, ¹⁷saying, "He gave me these six measures of barley, for he said, 'Do not go back to your mother-in-law empty-handed.' "

4:1–8

1 No sooner had Boaz gone up to the gate and sat down there than the next-of-kin, of whom Boaz had spoken, came passing by. So Boaz said, "Come over, friend; sit down here." And he went over and sat down. ²Then Boaz took ten men of the elders of the city, and said, "Sit down here"; so they sat down. ³He then said to the next-of-kin, "Naomi, who has come back from the country of Moab, is selling the parcel of land that belonged to our kinsman Elimelech. ⁴So I thought I would tell you of it, and say: Buy it in the presence of those sitting here and in the presence

of the elders of my people. If you will redeem it, redeem it; but if you will not, tell me, so that I may know; for there is no one prior to you to redeem it, and I come after you." So he said, "I will redeem it." ⁵Then Boaz said, "The day you acquire the field from the hand of Naomi, you are also acquiring Ruth the Moabite, the widow of the dead man, to maintain the dead man's name on his inheritance." ⁶At this, the next-of-kin said, "I cannot redeem it for myself without damaging my own inheritance. Take my right of redemption yourself, for I cannot redeem it."

7 Now this was the custom in former times in Israel concerning a redeeming and exchanging: to confirm a transaction, the one took off a sandal and gave it to the other; this was the manner of attesting in Israel. ⁸So when the next-of-kin said to Boaz, "Acquire it for yourself," he took off his sandal.

4:11–22

11 Then all the people who were at the gate, along with the elders, said, "We are witnesses. May the Lord make the woman who is coming into your house like Rachel and Leah, who together built up the house of Israel. May you produce children in Ephrathah and bestow a name in Bethlehem; ¹²and, through the children that the Lord will give you by this young woman, may your house be like the house of Perez, whom Tamar bore to Judah."

13 So Boaz took Ruth and she became his wife. When they came together, the Lord made her conceive, and she bore a son. ¹⁴Then the women said to Naomi, "Blessed be the Lord, who has not left you this day without next-of-kin; and may his name be renowned in Israel! ¹⁵He shall be to you a restorer of life and a nourisher of your old age; for your daughter-in-law who loves you, who is more to you than seven sons, has borne him." ¹⁶Then Naomi took the child and laid him in her bosom, and became his nurse. ¹⁷The women of the neighborhood gave him a name, saying, "A son has been born to Naomi." They named him Obed; he became the father of Jesse, the father of David.

18 Now these are the descendants of Perez: Perez became the father of Hezron, ¹⁹Hezron of Ram, Ram of Amminadab, ²⁰Amminadab of Nahshon, Nahshon of Salmon, ²¹Salmon of Boaz, Boaz of Obed, ²²Obed of Jesse, and Jesse of David.

THE STORY OF BATHSHEBA

2 SAMUEL 11, 12

1 In the spring of the year, the time when kings go out to battle, David sent Joab with his officers and all Israel with him; they

ravaged the Ammonites, and besieged Rabbah. But David remained at Jerusalem.

2 It happened, late one afternoon, when David rose from his couch and was walking about on the roof of the king's house, that he saw from the roof a woman bathing; the woman was very beautiful. [3]David sent someone to inquire about the woman. It was reported, "This is Bathsheba daughter of Eliam, the wife of Uriah the Hittite." [4]So David sent messengers to get her, and she came to him, and he lay with her. (Now she was purifying herself after her period.) Then she returned to her house. [5]The woman conceived; and she sent and told David, "I am pregnant."

6 So David sent word to Joab, "Send me Uriah the Hittite." And Joab sent Uriah to David. [7]When Uriah came to him, David asked how Joab and the people fared, and how the war was going. [8]Then David said to Uriah, "Go down to your house, and wash your feet." Uriah went out of the king's house, and there followed him a present from the king. [9]But Uriah slept at the entrance of the king's house with all the servants of his lord, and did not go down to his house. [10]When they told David, "Uriah did not go down to his house," David said to Uriah, "You have just come from a journey. Why did you not go down to your house?" [11]Uriah said to David, "The ark and Israel and Judah remain in booths; and my lord Joab and the servants of my lord are camping in the open field; shall I then go to my house, to eat and to drink, and to lie with my wife? As you live, and as your soul lives, I will not do such a thing." [12]Then David said to Uriah, "Remain here today also, and tomorrow I will send you back." So Uriah remained in Jerusalem that day. On the next day, [13]David invited him to eat and drink in his presence and made him drunk; and in the evening he went out to lie on his couch with the servants of his lord, but he did not go down to his house.

14 In the morning David wrote a letter to Joab, and sent it by the hand of Uriah. [15]In the letter he wrote, "Set Uriah in the forefront of the hardest fighting, and then draw back from him, so that he may be struck down and die." [16]As Joab was besieging the city, he assigned Uriah to the place where he knew there were valiant warriors. [17]The men of the city came out and fought with Joab; and some of the servants of David among the people fell. Uriah the Hittite was killed as well. [18]Then Joab sent and told David all the news about the fighting; [19]and he instructed

the messenger, "When you have finished telling the king all the news about the fighting, ²⁰then, if the king's anger rises, and if he says to you, 'Why did you go so near the city to fight? Did you not know that they would shoot from the wall? ²¹Who killed Abimelech son of Jerubbaal? Did not a woman throw an upper millstone on him from the wall, so that he died at Thebez? Why did you go so near the wall?' then you shall say, 'Your servant Uriah the Hittite is dead too.' "

22 So the messenger went, and came and told David all that Joab had sent him to tell. ²³The messenger said to David, "The men gained an advantage over us, and came out against us in the field; but we drove them back to the entrance of the gate. ²⁴Then the archers shot at your servants from the wall; some of the king's servants are dead; and your servant Uriah the Hittite is dead also." ²⁵David said to the messenger, "Thus you shall say to Joab, 'Do not let this matter trouble you, for the sword devours now one and now another; press your attack on the city, and overthrow it.' And encourage him."

26 When the wife of Uriah heard that her husband was dead, she made lamentation for him. ²⁷When the mourning was over, David sent and brought her to his house, and she became his wife, and bore him a son.

But the thing that David had done displeased the Lord, ¹and the Lord sent Nathan to David. He came to him, and said to him, "There were two men in a certain city, the one rich and the other poor. ²The rich man had very many flocks and herds; ³but the poor man had nothing but one little ewe lamb, which he had bought. He brought it up, and it grew up with him and with his children; it used to eat of his meager fare, and drink from his cup, and lie in his bosom, and it was like a daughter to him. ⁴Now there came a traveler to the rich man, and he was loath to take one of his own flock or herd to prepare for the wayfarer who had come to him, but he took the poor man's lamb, and prepared that for the guest who had come to him." ⁵Then David's anger was greatly kindled against the man. He said to Nathan, "As the Lord lives, the man who has done this deserves to die; ⁶he shall restore the lamb fourfold, because he did this thing, and because he had no pity."

7 Nathan said to David, "You are the man! Thus says the Lord, the God of Israel: I anointed you king over Israel, and I rescued you from the hand of Saul; ⁸I gave you your master's house, and your master's wives into your bosom, and gave you the house of

Israel and of Judah; and if that had been too little, I would have added as much more. ⁹Why have you despised the word of the Lord, to do what is evil in his sight? You have struck down Uriah the Hittite with the sword, and have taken his wife to be your wife, and have killed him with the sword of the Ammonites. ¹⁰Now therefore the sword shall never depart from your house, for you have despised me, and have taken the wife of Uriah the Hittite to be your wife. ¹¹Thus says the Lord: I will raise up trouble against you from within your own house; and I will take your wives before your eyes, and give them to your neighbor, and he shall lie with your wives in the sight of this very sun. ¹²For you did it secretly; but I will do this thing before all Israel, and before the sun." ¹³David said to Nathan, "I have sinned against the Lord." Nathan said to David, "Now the Lord has put away your sin; you shall not die. ¹⁴Nevertheless, because by this deed you have utterly scorned the Lord, the child that is born to you shall die." ¹⁵Then Nathan went to his house.

The Lord struck the child that Uriah's wife bore to David, and it became very ill. ¹⁶David therefore pleaded with God for the child; David fasted, and went in and lay all night on the ground. ¹⁷The elders of his house stood beside him, urging him to rise from the ground; but he would not, nor did he eat food with them. ¹⁸On the seventh day the child died. And the servants of David were afraid to tell him that the child was dead; for they said, "While the child was still alive, we spoke to him, and he did not listen to us; how then can we tell him the child is dead? He may do himself some harm." ¹⁹But when David saw that his servants were whispering together, he perceived that the child was dead; and David said to his servants, "Is the child dead?" They said, "He is dead."

20 Then David rose from the ground, washed, anointed himself, and changed his clothes. He went into the house of the Lord, and worshiped; he then went to his own house; and when he asked, they set food before him and he ate. ²¹Then his servants said to him, "What is this thing that you have done? You fasted and wept for the child while it was alive; but when the child died, you rose and ate food." ²²He said, "While the child was still alive, I fasted and wept; for I said, 'Who knows? The Lord may be gracious to me, and the child may live.' ²³But now he is dead; why should I fast? Can I bring him back again? I shall go to him, but he will not return to me."

24 Then David consoled his wife Bathsheba, and went to her, and

lay with her; and she bore a son, and he named him Solomon. The Lord loved him, ²⁵and sent a message by the prophet Nathan; so he named him Jedidiah, because of the Lord.

26 Now Joab fought against Rabbah of the Ammonites, and took the royal city. ²⁷Joab sent messengers to David, and said, "I have fought against Rabbah; moreover, I have taken the water city. ²⁸Now, then, gather the rest of the people together, and encamp against the city, and take it; or I myself will take the city, and it will be called by my name." ²⁹So David gathered all the people together and went to Rabbah, and fought against it and took it. ³⁰He took the crown of Milcom from his head; the weight of it was a talent of gold, and in it was a precious stone; and it was placed on David's head. He also brought forth the spoil of the city, a very great amount. ³¹He brought out the people who were in it, and set them to work with saws and iron picks and iron axes, or sent them to the brickworks. Thus he did to all the cities of the Ammonites. Then David and all the people returned to Jerusalem.

I KINGS 1:11–21

11 Then Nathan said to Bathsheba, Solomon's mother, "Have you not heard that Adonijah son of Haggith has become king and our lord David does not know it? ¹²Now therefore come, let me give you advice, so that you may save your own life and the life of your son Solomon. ¹³Go in at once to King David, and say to him, 'Did you not, my lord the king, swear to your servant, saying: Your son Solomon shall succeed me as king, and he shall sit on my throne? Why then is Adonijah king?' ¹⁴Then while you are still there speaking with the king, I will come in after you and confirm your words."

15 So Bathsheba went to the king in his room. The king was very old; Abishag the Shunammite was attending the king. ¹⁶Bathsheba bowed and did obeisance to the king, and the king said, "What do you wish?" ¹⁷She said to him, "My lord, you swore to your servant by the Lord your God, saying: Your son Solomon shall succeed me as king, and he shall sit on my throne. ¹⁸But now suddenly Adonijah has become king, though you, my lord the king, do not know it. ¹⁹He has sacrificed oxen, fatted cattle, and sheep in abundance, and has invited all the children of the king, the priest Abiathar, and Joab the commander of the army; but your servant Solomon he has not invited. ²⁰But you, my lord the king—the eyes of all Israel are on you to tell them

who shall sit on the throne of my lord the king after him. ²¹Otherwise it will come to pass, when my lord the king sleeps with his ancestors, that my son Solomon and I will be counted offenders."

1:28–31

28 King David answered, "Summon Bathsheba to me." So she came into the king's presence, and stood before the king. ²⁹The king swore, saying, "As the Lord lives, who has saved my life from every adversity, ³⁰as I swore to you by the Lord, the God of Israel, 'Your son Solomon shall succeed me as king, and he shall sit on my throne in my place,' so will I do this day." ³¹Then Bathsheba bowed with her face to the ground, and did obeisance to the king, and said, "May my lord King David live forever!"

2:13–21

13 Then Adonijah son of Haggith came to Bathsheba, Solomon's mother. She asked, "Do you come peaceably?" He said, "Peaceably." ¹⁴Then he said, "May I have a word with you?" She said, "Go on." ¹⁵He said, "You know that the kingdom was mine, and that all Israel expected me to reign; however, the kingdom has turned about and become my brother's, for it was his from the Lord. ¹⁶And now I have one request to make of you; do not refuse me." She said to him, "Go on." ¹⁷He said, "Please ask King Solomon—he will not refuse you—to give me Abishag the Shunammite as my wife." ¹⁸Bathsheba said, "Very well; I will speak to the king on your behalf."

19 So Bathsheba went to King Solomon, to speak to him on behalf of Adonijah. The king rose to meet her, and bowed down to her; then he sat on his throne, and had a throne brought for the king's mother, and she sat on his right. ²⁰Then she said, "I have one small request to make of you; do not refuse me." And the king said to her, "Make your request, my mother; for I will not refuse you." ²¹She said, "Let Abishag the Shunammite be given to your brother Adonijah as his wife."

I CHRONICLES 3:5–8

⁵These were born to him in Jerusalem: Shimea, Shobab, Nathan, and Solomon, four by Bath-shua, daughter of Ammiel; ⁶then Ibhar, Elishama, Eliphelet, ⁷Nogah, Nepheg, Japhia, ⁸Elishama, Eliada, and Eliphelet, nine.

INDEX

C. G. JUNG FOUNDATION BOOKS

Absent Fathers, Lost Sons: The Search for Masculine Identity, by Guy Corneau.

Closeness in Personal and Professional Relationships, edited by Harry A. Wilmer. Foreword by Maya Angelou.

Cross-Currents of Jungian Thought: An Annotated Bibliography, by Donald R. Dyer.

*Dreams, by Marie-Louise von Franz.

Ego and Archetype: Individuation and the Religious Function of the Psyche, by Edward F. Edinger.

The Female Ancestors of Christ, by Ann Belford Ulanov.

The Feminine in Fairy Tales, Revised Edition, by Marie-Louise von Franz.

*From Freud to Jung: A Comparative Study of the Psychology of the Unconscious, by Liliane Frey-Rohn. Foreword by Robert Hinshaw.

Gathering the Light: A Psychology of Meditation, by V. Walter Odajnyk.

The Golden Ass of Apuleius: The Liberation of the Feminine in Man, by Marie-Louise von Franz.

A Guided Tour of the Collected Works *of C. G. Jung*, by Robert H. Hopcke. Foreword by Aryeh Maidenbaum.

In Her Image: The Unhealed Daughter's Search for Her Mother, by Kathie Carlson.

*The Inner Child in Dreams, by Kathrin Asper.

The Inner Lover, by Valerie Harms.

Knowing Woman: A Feminine Psychology, by Irene Claremont de Castillejo.

Lingering Shadows: Jungians, Freudians, and Anti-Semitism, edited by Aryeh Maidenbaum and Stephen A. Martin.

Masculinity: Identity, Conflict, and Transformation, by Warren Steinberg.

The Old Wise Woman: A Study of Active Imagination, by Rix Weaver. Introduction by C. A. Meier.

Power and Politics: The Psychology of Soviet-American Partnership, by Jerome S. Bernstein. Forewords by Senator Claiborne Pell and Edward C. Whitmont, M.D.

*Psyche and Matter, by Marie-Louise von Franz.

*Psychotherapy, by Marie-Louise von Franz.

The Way of All Women, by M. Esther Harding. Introduction by C. G. Jung.

The Wisdom of the Dream: The World of C. G. Jung, by Stephen Segaller and Merrill Berger.

Witches, Ogres, and the Devil's Daughter: Encounters with Evil in Fairy Tales, by Mario Jacoby, Verena Kast, and Ingrid Riedel.

*Published in association with Daimon Verlag, Einsiedeln, Switzerland.